PRENTICE-HALL
FOUNDATIONS OF MODERN SOCIOLOGY SERIES

PRENTICE-HALL
FOUNDATIONS OF MODERN SOCIOLOGY SERIES

Alex Inkeles, Editor

THE SCIENTIST'S ROLE IN SOCIETY
Joseph Ben-David

DEVIANCE AND CONTROL
Albert K. Cohen

MODERN ORGANIZATIONS
Amitai Etzioni

THE FAMILY
William J. Goode

SOCIETY AND POPULATION, Second Edition
David M. Heer

WHAT IS SOCIOLOGY? An Introduction to the Discipline and Profession
Alex Inkeles

THE SOCIOLOGY OF SMALL GROUPS
Theodore M. Mills

SOCIAL CHANGE, Second Edition
Wilbert E. Moore

THE SOCIOLOGY OF RELIGION
Thomas F. O'Dea

SOCIETIES: Evolutionary and Comparative Perspectives
Talcott Parsons

THE SYSTEM OF MODERN SOCIETIES
Talcott Parsons

THE AMERICAN SCHOOL: A Sociological Analysis
Patricia C. Sexton

THE SOCIOLOGY OF ECONOMIC LIFE
Neil J. Smelser

SOCIAL STRATIFICATION: The Forms and Functions of Inequality
Melvin M. Tumin

SOCIETY AND POPULATION

second edition

SOCIETY AND POPULATION

DAVID M. HEER
University of Southern California

Prentice-Hall, Inc., Englewood Cliffs, New Jersey

Library of Congress Cataloging in Publication Data

HEER, DAVID M
  Society and population.

  (Prentice-Hall foundations of modern sociology series)
  Includes bibliographical references and index.
  1. Population. 2. Demography. I. Title.
HB851.H4 1975   301.32   74-20727
ISBN 0-13-820712-7
ISBN 0-13-820704-6 pbk.

Printed in the United States of America

10 9 8 7 6 5 4 3 2 1

Prentice-Hall International, Inc., London
Prentice-Hall of Australia, Pty. Ltd., Sydney
Prentice-Hall of Canada, Ltd., Toronto
Prentice-Hall of India Private Limited, New Delhi
Prentice-Hall of Japan, Inc., Tokyo

In memory of Samuel A. Stouffer, who combined deep interest
in social theory with uncommon competence to test its veracity

CONTENTS

PREFACE

This book is intended both to reveal some of the ways in which an understanding of population is important to a proper study of sociology, and to help explain the causes and effects of the current "population explosion."

I have long felt that too many books (in all fields of study) fail to stimulate their readers because they overemphasize what is already known, and hardly bother with important questions which deserve to be—indeed, in some cases *must* be—answered. Only by arousing his readers' curiosity concerning *both* sides of the subject at hand—the unknown *as well as* the known—will an author get them to take that all-important first step along the path of intellectual inquiry. In this book I have tried to determine what are the important questions concerning population, and how well we can answer them so far. Anyone completing this book will realize how much room exists for further significant research.

Textbooks on population traditionally devote considerable space to describing the social composition of populations such as the distribution of populations by marital and family status, educational attainment, ethnicity, language, religion, labor-force status, occupation, industry, and income. For reasons of space, I have eliminated this rather lengthy topic and have confined the discussion of population composition to biological composition. Thus, age and sex composition are discussed rather thoroughly, and brief mention is made of genetic composition in a discussion of differential reproduction and intelligence. Furthermore, this book is focused on the populations of nation-states and of the world as a whole; no attempt is made to consider population structure and dynamics for other types of social systems. Thus we do not consider divorce, which in demographic terms represents out-migration from that social system we term "the family." In addition, we are not concerned with the population processes of strata within a society—for example, entrances to and exits from the labor force, the body of college graduates, or a particular socio-economic class. Nor do we treat the geographic distribution of social strata; hence we shall not pursue such topics as the residential segregation of whites from blacks in American cities. The social composition of the population of the United States and of other societies, the influence of population structure and dynamics on social systems other than societies, and the population structure of various social strata within societies are, of course, common topics of sudy for sociologists. Much data relating to these topics will be found in the other volumes of the Foundations of Modern Sociology Series.

I should like to express my appreciation to all those persons who have helped in the preparation of this book: to Alex Inkeles, the General Editor of the Prentice-Hall Foundations of Modern Sociology Series, who made valuable suggestions concerning the organization of this work; to the staff of Prentice-Hall, Inc.; and to Miss Linda Sayegh, Miss Dorothy Greenidge, and Mrs. Margaret Bermingham, who typed successive drafts of the manuscript.

Davɪᴅ M. Heer

SOCIETY AND POPULATION

PART ONE
THE WORLD POPULATION PICTURE

CHAPTER 1
THE GROWTH
OF WORLD
POPULATION

THE HISTORY OF HUMAN
POPULATION GROWTH

When one considers that even today we do not know with certainty the actual size of populations in many parts of the world, it is not surprising to discover that we have only approximate knowledge (which often means "the results of educated guesses") concerning the number of human beings living at each stage of man's existence. On the basis of careful analyses of available fact, however, we are very sure of one aspect of the expansion of man's numbers: it has been truly prodigious.

In considering the history of human population growth we must first decide what we mean by "man." *Man* obviously is the descendant of other primates, but as yet we have no clear picture of all the links between him and his prehominid ancestors. Moreover, even if all the links were apparent, we would still have the problem of defining when "man" himself appeared. For instance, do we wish to define the appearance of man as the appearance of the family *hominidae,* the genus *homo,* or the species *homo sapiens?* If we choose to trace the population history of the family *hominidae,* we may have to go back 5½ million years; if we confine our interest to *homo sapiens,* we need go back only around 50,000 years.

Perhaps the most important stage in the evolution of man from other primates was the appearance of terrestrial, rather than tree-dwelling, creatures of fully upright posture who were able not only to use tools but also to make them. All such creatures are classed in the family *hominidae*. The first creatures to fit definitely into this category, who now bear the technical name *Australopithecines*, developed during the geological epoch before ours (the *Pleistocene*) perhaps as long as $5\frac{1}{2}$ million years ago. The *Australopithecine*, an organism of completely upright posture, was free to use his flexible hands to grasp weapons for hunting other animals. Thus for the first time a mammal evolved which was dependent on tools for survival.[1]

The development of tools for hunting enabled the creatures who used them to expand their population in a slowly accelerating fashion. Deevey estimates that 1 million years ago there were only 125,000 tool-using hominid creatures, but that by 8000 B.C. the population of *homo sapiens*, by then the only hominid, was 5.3 million and growing fast.[2] According to Deevey, a population boom of sorts began around 8000 B.C. that caused about a sixteenfold increase over the next 4,000 years. Translated, this statistic means that the earth harbored a population of around 86.5 million in 4000 B.C., the approximate date of the rise of the First Egyptian Empire in the Nile Valley.

Population seems to have grown less rapidly in the following 4,000 years. Deevey estimates that at the time of Christ the population of the world was 133 million, less than a twofold increase over that of the preceding four millennia. However, there is disagreement on this point by other scholars. The United Nations, for example, reports that the population of the world at this time was between 200 million and 300 million.[3]

By 1650 A.D. the population of the world had probably risen to about 545 million. Since that date, as Table 1 shows, there has been a continually accelerating increase. According to the most recent official estimate of the United Nations, the latest recorded average annual rate of population growth (from 1963 to 1971) was 20 per thousand.[4] Some population experts believe the rate to be even higher. Accordingly, it is

1.   Frederick S. Hulse, *The Human Species* (New York: Random House, 1963), pp. 164–235; Robert Reinhold, "Bone Traces Man Back 5 Million Years", *New York Times*, 19 February 1971.

2.   Edward S. Deevey, Jr., "The Human Population," *Scientific American* (September, 1960), 203: 3, 195–204.

3.   Population Division, United Nations, *The Determinants and Consequences of Population Trends* (New York: United Nations, 1953), p. 8.

4.   Estimates of population and growth-rates from 1650 to 1900 are from A. M. Carr-Saunders, *World Population: Past Growth and Present Trends* (Oxford: Clarendon, 1936), p. 42. The growth rate from 1900 to 1950 is based on Carr-Saunders's estimate of world population for 1900 and the United Nations' estimate of world population for 1950. The source of the latter is United Nations, Department of Economic and Social Affairs, *Demographic Yearbook, 1971* (New York: United

Table 1   Estimated Population of the World since 1650

YEAR	POPULATION (IN MILLIONS)	AVERAGE ANNUAL INCREASE PER 1,000 SINCE PRECEDING DATE
1650	545	—
1750	728	3
1800	906	4
1850	1,171	5
1900	1,608	6
1950	2,486	9
1963	3,162	19
1971	3,706	20

Sources: See footnote 4.

very clear that in recent years the rate of population growth the world over has been unprecedented in human history.

This recent increase in population has not been *uniformly* great, however; the highest rates of increase have been found in the tropical parts of Latin America. Brazil, with about 95 million persons in 1971, was growing at a rate of 28 persons per thousand during the period 1963–71; Mexico, with about 51 million persons in 1971, was growing at a rate of 32 per thousand. Population growth substantially higher than the world average was also reported for Africa, whose growth rate for the 1963–71 period was reported as 26 per thousand per year.

Population growth rates lower than the world average during the 1963–71 period were found in Europe, the United States, Japan, and the USSR. During 1963–71 the average annual rate of population growth was 11 per thousand in the United States and 8 per thousand in Europe. During this period the lowest rates of population growth were for East Germany (− 1 per thousand) and for the United Kingdom, Hungary, and Finland (4 per thousand).[5] The population growth rate in mainland China, containing about a fifth of the world's population, is uncertain. The United Nations has recently estimated that the average annual population growth rate in mainland China from 1963 to 1971 was 18 per thousand.[6] Other experts on Chinese population,[7] however, believe the

---

Nations, 1972), p. 111. The estimates of world population in 1963 and 1971 are also taken from p. 111.

5. United Nations, Department of Economic and Social Affairs, *Demographic Yearbook, 1971*, pp. 111–124.

6. Ibid.

7. John S. Aird, "Population Policy and Demographic Prospects in the People's Republic of China," in Joint Economic Committee, Congress of the United States,

growth rate was substantially higher. In fact, the uncertainty concerning the growth rate in China is the main cause of the uncertainty about the world growth rate.

TWO FRAMEWORKS FOR ANALYZING
THE CAUSES OF POPULATION GROWTH

Two separate frameworks of causal explanation are available for explaining world population growth. The first framework relates population to the means of subsistence. It is obvious that the population of the world can be no greater than that number which can provide itself with a minimum subsistence from the world's resources. Since for most of the period in which human beings have inhabited this planet, the majority have lived very close to a minimum level of subsistence, major population increase has only been possible when the means of subsistence could be increased proportionately.

A second framework for examining the causes of world population increase is the examination of this increase in terms of its two components, the birth rate and the death rate. On a worldwide basis, population cannot increase unless the birth rate exceeds the death rate, and the greater the difference between the two rates (in favor of births, of course), the higher will be the rate of population growth. Analysis of world population growth from the standpoint of this framework focuses on factors leading to *changes* in birth and death rates.

Population Growth and the
Means of Subsistence

Societies develop because no human being can grow to maturity independently of others of his species. Human societies are in turn dependent on other animals, on plant species, and on such requisite features of the inanimate environment as water, air, and proper temperature. Human ecology is the study of the mutual relationships existing between human populations and their biological and physical environments. A key concept of human ecology is the *ecosystem*, which may be defined as "an aggregation of associated species of plants and animals together with the physical features of their habitat."[8] The past growth of world popula-

---

People's Republic of China: An Economic Assessment (Washington, D.C.: Government Printing Office, 1972).

8. Lee R. Dice, *Man's Nature and Nature's Man: The Ecology of Human Communities* (Ann Arbor, Mich.: University of Michigan Press, 1955), p. 2.

tion would not have been possible without mankind's making radical changes in his ecosystem. And these changes have not been merely quantitative; that is, modern man's relationship to his biological and physical environment is much more than an enlarged replication of the relationship of primitive man to his environment. Because of what economists call "the law of diminishing returns," the additional supply of labor occasioned by an increase in population usually results in *less* productivity than the existing labor supply. Hence, in the usual case, the means of subsistence do not automatically increase in proportion to a population increase. The mechanism by which man's means of subsistence have kept abreast of growing population is a *qualitative* change in his ecosystem—namely, a change in technology and organization serving to increase the production possible on a given amount of territory with a given quantity of labor.

A most useful way of explaining world population increase since the beginning of man's existence has been developed by Walter Goldschmidt.[9] Essentially a typology of the evolution of societies in terms of the complexity of their technology and the elaboration of their division of labor, it chronicles the improvements in technology and organization which have helped mankind to increase the total output of his necessities. According to Goldschmidt, the first type of society to evolve was one in which the predominant economic activity was nomadic hunting and food-gathering. This was followed by the development of a society in which hunting and food-gathering could take place without nomadism. The third stage of complexity consisted of societies in which the predominant economic activity was either horticulture (i.e., the cultivation of plants by means of the hoe) or the herding of animals. The fourth stage was characterized by a fully developed agriculture and the accumulation of a sufficient agricultural surplus to allow for the settlement of a portion of the population in cities. The fifth, and so far final, stage is one in which the division of labor becomes very complex, subsistence is obtained largely through the application of inanimate sources of energy (such as coal and petroleum), and much or most of the population lives in cities. Each type of society progressively allows a population of given size to procure a greater supply of goods and services from a given territory, and thus each societal type progressively allows for a higher density of population. In fact, as actual societies have progressed upward along this typology, *all* of them have experienced increased population density.

Goldschmidt's typology would seem to imply a certain discontinuity in the evolution of more efficient systems of sustenance, and hence in population growth. However, he merely intends the five-stage breakdown

9. Walter Goldschmidt, *Man's Way* (Cleveland, Ohio: World, 1959), pp. 181–218.

as a device to emphasize certain major changes without implying that the changes summarized by a given type appeared all at once.

Let us examine in somewhat more detail some of the major technological and organizational developments which have affected man's ability to support given population densities at each of the several stages. If we begin our account with the earliest representatives of the family *hominidae*, we can presume that the use of fire was unknown and that their language was extremely rudimentary. The "harnessing" of fire and the development of language undoubtedly allowed for an increase in the hominid population. So also did the improvement of tools for hunting. The spear, for example, was more efficient than the club, and the bow and arrow more efficient than the spear. Inventions such as these enabled men to evolve from small, nomadic hunting bands to more settled tribal societies. The invention of the hoe and the primitive cultivation of plants allowed for a major increase in subsistence, and thus had a profound effect on human population growth. Deevey, who as we have seen estimates that the world population increased sixteenfold in the period from 8000 B.C. to 4000 B.C., attributes this large increase to the development of horticulture and the beginnings of a more advanced agriculture.

The fourth type of society, the agricultural-state society, emerged around 4000 B.C. in the Nile delta of Egypt, the Tigris-Euphrates Valley in Iraq, the Indus Valley in Pakistan, and the Yellow and Yangtze valleys in China. The agricultural-state society is characterized above all by the presence of domesticated animals, the use of the plow, and the irrigation of agricultural land wherever possible. In addition, other technological developments, such as terracing, fertilizers, wheeled vehicles, sailboats, metallurgy, and the alphabet, date from this period, and all contributed to increased productivity. The domestication of animals allowed for a specialized herding society in certain steppe regions which were unsuitable for other types of agriculture. Such herding societies, although evolving later than horticultural societies, are of the same level of complexity, and hence have been classified by Goldschmidt as belonging in the third stage of development.

The fifth stage is the urban-industrial stage. Its beginnings in Europe may be said to coincide with Christopher Columbus's voyage to America. The voyages to the New World by Columbus and the other early discoverers were significant to technological advance for two reasons. First, the explorers brought back certain very important cultivated plants previously unknown in Europe and Asia. Among these were the potato, maize, beans, and tomatoes. Of these plants, probably the most important to Northern Europe was the potato, because the cool and rainy summers of that region are not so fitted to grain production as are warmer climates. The potato, although not native to the region, was ideally suited to it, and the produce of potatoes from one acre of land was equivalent in food value to that of two to four acres sown with grain. The potato was introduced into Ireland around 1600, and probably had its greatest impact there. By 1800 the potato was practically the sole item in the diet of the Irish common man. Meanwhile, a tremendous acceleration in population occurred: from 1754 to 1846 the population of Ireland more than doubled, increasing from 3.2 million to 8.2 million, despite heavy out-migration to the United States and other nations. The potato played an equally important role, although at a somewhat later date, in the other countries of Northern Europe—particularly in England, the Netherlands, Scandinavia, Germany, Poland, and Russia. In Russia, from 1725 to 1858 the population increased more than threefold (within the boundaries of the former year), an increase parallel in magnitude to the increase in population in Ireland.[10]

The second reason for the significance of Columbus's voyage was that it made possible a tremendous technical advance in America. First of all, the European introduction to America of the horse and other domesticated animals was a major innovation which allowed the indigenous population of America to increase greatly its means of subsistence. For example, the Indians of the Great Plains of North America, by using horses, were for the first time able to live off bison. Secondly, and more important, the Europeans had a much higher level of technology than the American Indians, particularly those Indians in what is now the United States and Canada; and by virtue of taking over territory from the Indians, the European settlers converted a very large territory from one in which the population had only a very simple technology to one whose technology was as advanced as any in the world. As a result, the population of the New World could and did grow extremely rapidly.

A major landmark of the urban-industrial stage was the invention of the steam engine by James Watt in 1769. This invention signalled the beginning of the period in which man's major supply of energy was to come from inanimate fossilized sources (coal, petroleum, and natural gas). As a result of numerous inventions, the efficient use of inanimate energy was greatly stimulated in Europe, North America, and elsewhere. We shall not go into these many inventions in detail; it will be sufficient to state two rather broad consequences of them which affected possibilities for population growth. First, a series of innovations in agriculture and manufacturing made it possible for a rapidly decreasing number of persons to produce an increasing quantity of food, clothing, shelter, and

10. William L. Langer, "Europe's Initial Population Explosion," *The American Historical Review* (October, 1963), 69:1, 1–17.

other necessities from the resources of a given area. Secondly, a revolution in the costs of transportation made it possible for different regions to specialize in those goods and services which they could produce at the lowest cost and eliminated the danger of famine caused by local failures in food production.

Although population growth was stimulated in Europe and America by the Industrial Revolution, the advance in the means of subsistence was substantially greater. Hence, for the first time in human history, certain nations experienced a rapid rise in their level of living. For example, in the United States the total output of goods and services (GNP—gross national product) per capita in constant prices increased on the average during the period from 1839 to 1959 by 1.64 percent per annum. Such an increase meant a doubling in per-capita product every forty-three years, and approximately a fivefold increase every century.[11]

As we have seen, an advancing technology and an increasing division of labor allow population to increase, and insofar as advance in technology and organization stimulate a rise in birth rate or a decline in death rate, such an advance causes population growth. However, we should also examine the other side of this relationship. Does increased population growth advance the state of technology and elaborate the division of labor? An argument by the famous French sociologist Emile Durkheim is to this effect.[12] Durkheim contends that an increase in population density is causally related to a more elaborate and productive division of labor. According to his argument, there is a natural tendency for population to expand more rapidly than the means of subsistence, and this expansion tends to sharpen the struggle for existence. Two alternatives are then possible: either men fight among themselves for the available means of subsistence, or they elaborate the division of labor to attain greater productivity. Since men have not consistently chosen the first of these two alternatives, the division of labor in human societies has become increasingly complex. Few persons would care to dispute the claim that population pressure is a contributing cause to an increasingly complex division of labor. Durkheim, however, holds that an elaboration of the division of labor can occur *only in the presence* of population pressure, and the validity of this conclusion is dubious. Durkheim's contention that population pressure is a necessary prerequisite to further development of the division of labor is, however, similar to that of certain contemporary scholars who believe that economic development will

---

11.   Richard T. Gill, *Economic Development: Past and Present* (Englewood Cliffs, N.J.: Prentice-Hall, 1967), p. 66.

12.   Emile Durkheim, *The Division of Labor in Society*, trans. George Simpson (New York: The Free Press, 1964), pp. 233–82.

not be hampered by a high rate of population growth. We shall consider their ideas in chapter 8.

Population Growth and Changes in Birth and Death Rates

The second framework for analyzing population growth concerns the factors that influence the rate of births and deaths. When compared with that of other animals, man's biological capacity to reproduce is rather limited. Unlike other animals, *homo sapiens* does not lay thousands of eggs, or typically bear offspring in litters. In the human population, women who live to the end of their reproductive period are capable of bearing only about twelve children on the average. Even so, few indeed have been (or are) the populations wherein women have ever reproduced (or still reproduce) at the level of their biological capacity. (The only such populations with which the average reader can be expected to be familiar involve the women of colonial North America who, both in French-speaking Quebec and in the English-speaking colonies of the Atlantic seaboard, reproduced at or near the level of maximum biological capacity; and the present Hutterite women, members of a small, communalistic Christian sect of the western United States and Canada, who have a similar high birth rate.)[13] Currently, the economically developed nations generaly have much lower fertility than the economically less advanced nations. Nevertheless, in all nations today fertility is substantially lower than the biological maximum.

On a worldwide level up until perhaps 300 years ago, the birth rate and the death rate were both very high, and each averaged to a level almost exactly equal to the other. Thus, if the death rate averaged around 50 per thousand, the birth rate would also average that amount. Of course, in any given year birth rates and death rates would not be exactly equal; death rates in particular tended to vary considerably from year to year.

In years with an adequate food supply, population growth, at least

13. For a discussion of Hutterite fertility and its relation to biologically maximum fertility, see J. W. Eaton and A. J. Mayer, "The Social Biology of Very High Fertility among the Hutterites," *Human Biology* (1953), 25, pp. 206–63; Christopher Tietze, "Reproductive Span and Rate of Reproduction among Hutterite Women," *Fertility and Sterility* (1957), 8:1, 89–97; and Mindel C. Sheps, "An Analysis of Reproductive Patterns in an American Isolate," *Population Studies*, 19:1 (July, 1965), pp. 65–80. For a discussion of fertility in the colonial United States, see Wilson H. Grabill et al., *The Fertility of American Women* (New York: John Wiley, 1958), pp. 5–24. Fertility in French-Canada during the early eighteenth century is discussed in Jacques Henripin, *La Population Canadienne au début du XVIIIe siècle: nuptialité, fécondité, mortalité infantile* (Paris: Presses Universitaires de France, 1954).

in agricultural societies, was about 5 or 10 per thousand.[14] Years of food scarcity tended to have very high death rates. Not only did food shortage sometimes cause actual starvation; more importantly, it caused malnutrition and undernourishment, and under these conditions the death rate from various infectious diseases rose markedly. One of the most famous epidemics in human history was the Black Death, which occurred in Europe during the years 1347–52. An epidemic of bubonic plague began in Constantinople in 1347 and spread throughout the Mediterranean region and the European Atlantic coast during the following year. It then moved inland and continued until it struck Russia in 1352. The Black Death killed approximately one-quarter of the population of Europe, and the continent was not able to regain its former population for many years.[15]

The birth rate in pre-industrial societies was more stable than the death rate. However, at least in pre-industrial Europe the level of the birth rate was indirectly affected by the death rate because of a direct influence of the death rate on the age at marriage. In much of Europe, marriage was linked to inheritance. Since a marriage could not be contracted until the couple acquired land, they often had to wait for the death of the bridegroom's father. Following a period with an abnormally high death rate, a greater proportion of men would find themselves inheritors of land, and the average age of inheritance would be low. More men marrying and a decline in the age at marriage would result in a relatively high level of fertility. On the other hand, during periods when the death rate was low, fewer men would inherit land, and those inheriting would do so only at a later age. As a result, marriage would be less frequent and at a later age, and fertility would decline.[16]

Since the advent of the urban-industrial era, sharp rises in the death rate have accompanied each major war. However, the scientific-industrial revolution has markedly reduced peacetime mortality throughout the world. It is believed that mortality in Europe began to decline very slowly in the eighteenth century, quite possibly as a result of the more ample diet occasioned by the introduction and diffusion of the potato. It was not until the late nineteenth century that mortality in Europe and the area of European settlement began to decline rapidly, and the speed of *that* decline probably was caused by a combination of

14. Carlo M. Cipolla, *The Economic History of World Population* (Baltimore, Md.: Penguin, 1962), p. 78.

15. William Petersen, *Population*, 2d ed. (New York: Macmillan, 1969), pp. 388–91.

16. Goran Ohlin, "Mortality, Marriage, and Growth in Pre-Industrial Societies," *Population Studies* (March, 1961), 14:3, 190–97.

factors which had to await a variety of other human developments before they came into being: (1) a rise in the level of nutrition; (2) greatly improved sanitation, especially in cities, because of improvements in sewage and water supply systems; (3) medical advance in the prevention of infectious disease through inoculation; and (4) medical advance in the cure of infectious disease, particularly through the use of antibiotics. Outside of the economically developed nations, death rates remained high until the end of World War II. After World War II, a very pronounced reduction of mortality in these nations—a reduction much more rapid than had ever occurred in Europe or the United States—became the chief cause of the large recent acceleration in the world growth rate. Nevertheless, the level of mortality in these nations still remains, with some notable exceptions, distinctly higher than that of the economically developed nations.[17]

The very rapid decline of mortality in the underdeveloped nations after World War II resulted in large measure from inoculation for infectious disease, reduction of malaria through DDT spraying, and the cure of infectious disease through antibiotics. However, a large proportion of persons in these nations were and continue to be malnourished and living in unsanitary conditions.

The nations experiencing economic advance from the scientific industrial revolution were characterized not only by declining mortality but also by a fall in fertility. The *theory of the demographic transition* has been advanced as a comprehensive explanation of the effects of economic development both on mortality and on fertility decline. The classic theory is as follows. The initial stage is one of elevated birth and death rates; and because the birth rate is only approximately equal to the death rate, the natural increase in population is just about nil. In the second stage, there is a high rate of population growth caused by a decline in the death rate which proceeds at a much faster pace than the decline in the birth rate. In the third stage, the rate of population growth is positive but of lesser magnitude than in the second stage; in this third stage, the birth rate is declining more rapidly than the death rate. In the final stage, population growth is small or negative, since a low birth rate now approximates in magnitude a low death rate.[18]

17. On the decline of mortality in Europe, see David V. Glass and D. E. C. Eversley, eds., *Population in History* (Chicago, Ill.: Aldine, 1965), and for a general discussion of trends in mortality in different areas of the world see Population Division, United Nations, *The Determinants and Consequences of Population Trends* (New York: United Nations, 1953), pp. 47–70.

18. See Warren S. Thompson, *Population and Peace in the Pacific* (Chicago, Ill.: University of Chicago Press, 1946), pp. 22–35; C. P. Blacker, "Stages in Population Growth," *Eugenics Review* (October, 1947), 39:3, 88–102; Kingsley Davis, *Human*

The writers who popularized the idea of the demographic transition emphasized the simultaneous occurrence of economic development, industrialization, and urbanization as causes of the initial decline in mortality and the secondary decline in fertility. The fall in mortality was very plausibly explained: economic development led to a rise in the standard of living, including a higher level of nutrition, better sanitary facilities, and improved medical care. The supposed impact of industrialization, urbanization, and economic development on fertility, however, was spelled out less clearly. Until rather recently, most demographers accepted these three factors as necessary and sufficient for fertility reduction but paid relatively little attention to the *exact* ways in which changes in these three factors would affect fertility.

The theory of the demographic transition, popularized just after the end of World War II, was congruent with all of the facts then known about mortality and fertility. In this immediate postwar period the known facts referred to the world demographic situation just before World War II, because the vital events occurring during and just after the war were heavily influenced by the war itself and were therefore considered abnormal. During the period just before World War II, the industrialized nations of Europe, North America, and Oceania all had such low fertility and mortality that their intrinsic natural increase was nil. All of these nations were therefore considered to be in the fourth and final stage of demographic transition. Moreover, the demographic history of all these industrialized nations appeared to confirm the theory of demographic transition. All of them had experienced major *secular* (very long-term) declines, both in mortality and in fertility, with the decline in mortality generally preceding the decline in fertility. Furthermore, if one looked at the nations of the world in cross-sectional perspective, all of the developed nations with low fertility and mortality were in great contrast with the underdeveloped nations, all experiencing high fertility and, most of them, high mortality.

In the years following World War II, however, events cast increasing doubt on the classic statement of the demographic transition with respect to fertility. Demographers with faith in the theory of the demographic transition could not at first believe that fertility in the United States was actually rising to a level higher than that which had existed before World War II. At first the observed postwar jump in the birth rate was explained by the birth of babies temporarily postponed because of World War II. When this factor was found inadequate to explain the postwar increase

---

Society (New York: Macmillan, 1949), pp. 603–8; and Frank W. Notestein, "The Economics of Population and Food Supplies," in *Proceedings of the Eighth International Conference of Agricultural Economists* (London: Oxford University Press, 1953), pp. 15–31.

in fertility, much attention was paid to the effect of changes in age at marriage and at child-bearing on annual measures of fertility. P. K. Whelpton showed that a decline in age at marriage and in the maternal age at which children were born could result in a temporary inflation of the annual fertility measures even though there was no change in the average number of children per woman completing the reproductive period.[19] Since after World War II, the United States did experience a pronounced decline in the age at marriage and in the intervals between marriage and the birth of each child, it could plausibly be argued that the size of completed families in the United States was not rising. Only by the late 1950s had sufficient data accumulated to prove conclusively that the size of completed families in the United States among recent marriage cohorts was significantly above the level attained by those women who were married in the decade before World War II.[20]

Demographers were then faced with the embarrassing situation that fertility in the United States had increased despite the supposed fact that fertility would not rise once the final stage of demographic transition had been reached. Moreover, fertility had risen in a period which saw increased industrialization, increased urbanization, and a dramatic rise in the level of economic development.

During the last few years, corroborating evidence has been produced from various historical periods in other societies of direct rather than inverse associations between economic development and the trend in fertility. For example, several historical demographers have recently produced evidence indicating that English fertility may well have increased during that nation's period of industrial development in the early nineteenth century,[21] and similar increases may have occurred in the Netherlands during its periods of commercial and industrial development.[22]

A summation of this evidence suggests that a more adequate theory of fertility transition must distinguish between direct and indirect effects of economic development. The direct effect of economic development

19. Pascal K. Whelpton, *Cohort Fertility: Native White Women in the United States* (Princeton, N.J.: Princeton University Press, 1954).

20. U.S. Bureau of the Census, "Fertility of the Population: March 1957," in *Current Population Reports*, Series P-20, No. 84 (8 August 1958).

21. J. T. Krause, "Some Implications of Recent Work in Historical Demography," *Comparative Studies in Society and History* (January, 1957), 1:2, 164–88; H. J. Habakkuk, "English Population in the Eighteenth Century," *Economic History Review* (December, 1953), 6:2, 117–33.

22. William Petersen, "The Demographic Transition in the Netherlands" *American Sociological Review* (June, 1960), 25:3, 334–47.

and the consequent increase in economic well-being is probably an increase in fertility. The observed long-range historical fact that increased economic development usually has resulted in a reduction in fertility must then be caused by indirect effects of economic development conducive to fertility reduction which outweigh the facilitating effect of economic development. Some of the most important of these indirect effects of economic development conducive to fertility decline may be a decline in infant and childhood mortality, an increase in demand for an educated labor force, the introduction of social-security systems, and an increase in population density. The reasons why these and other changes accompanying economic development foster fertility decline will be discussed in chapter 5.

CHAPTER 2
FUTURE HUMAN SOCIETIES AND THEIR ENVIRONMENTAL CONSTRAINTS

THE FUTURE GROWTH OF WORLD POPULATION

Although we do not know enough about world population to be able to predict its future growth, we can (and it will be instructive for our present purposes) *project* it, assuming a continuation of the probable growth rate during very recent years. A population projection is simply the arithmetic spelling out of certain assumptions concerning the way in which populations grow. In this projection we shall assume that the rate of population growth will remain constant at 20 per thousand to the year 2400. The fantastic results are presented in table 2.

A population growing at a constant rate such as the one we have imagined doubles itself in a fixed time-period. When the rate of increase is 20 per thousand, this doubling occurs every thirty-five years. At this rate of increase, every century the population increases approximately sevenfold.

From table 2 one may also examine the population densities which would occur in connection with our assumed rate. In 1971 the population per square mile of terrestrial area in the world (excluding polar regions but including inland waters) was 70.7.[1] By the year 2400 it would be 376,218.

1. Calculated from the data provided in United Nations, Department of Economic and Social Affairs, *Demographic Yearbook, 1971* (New York: United Nations, 1972), p. 111.

Table 2   Projection of World Population Assuming an Annual Increase of 20 per thousand

YEAR	POPULATION (IN BILLIONS)	PER SQUARE MILE
1971	3.71	70.7
1975	4.01	76.5
2000	6.62	126.2
2025	10.91	208.0
2050	17.99	343.0
2075	29.66	565.5
2100	48.91	932.6
2200	361.39	6,890.7
2300	2,670.32	50,915.6
2400	19,731.13	376,218.0

This last figure may be compared with certain current population densities. In 1970 Manhattan Island (New York County) had a density of 66,923 persons per square mile, the highest for any political unit in the United States. For the city of New York the population density then was 26,343, and for New York City and its surrounding suburbs (the New York urbanized area) it was 6,683. By comparison, the population density in the well-populated state of Massachusetts in 1970 was only 727 per square mile, and in the United States as a whole, a low 57.5.[2]

BALANCE BETWEEN FUTURE POPULATION GROWTH AND FUTURE INCREASES IN THE MEANS OF SUBSISTENCE

I have presented this population projection not because many students of population seriously believe that it will come to pass, but rather to show the inevitability of a decline in population growth sometime in the future. When it will come is a matter of opinion, but all experts appear to agree that the world will never have anywhere near the population that has been projected here for the year 2400. A decline in the growth rate may come about because human beings will voluntarily restrict their fertility. On the other hand, if the world birth rate is not reduced, the growth of world population may outstrip the growth in means of subsistence. If this happens, mankind's death rate must inevitably rise.

The question of whether mankind could avoid an increase in its

2.   U.S. Bureau of the Census, *United States Census of Population: 1970*, Final Report PC(1)-A1, pp. 52, 81, and 152 and Final Report PC(1)-A34, p. 21.

death rate as a consequence of population growing faster than the means of subsistence was initially raised by Thomas Robert Malthus in 1798 in his famous first essay on population.[3] In this initial study, Malthus concluded that avoiding a mortality rise would not be possible. The means of subsistence, he claimed, grew only at an *arithmetic* rate, whereas populations tended to grow at a *geometric* rate. When the imbalance between growth in the means of subsistence and in population became too great, factors such as hunger, epidemic disease, and war—which Malthus termed *"positive checks"*—would operate to raise the death rate and reduce the population to a level compatible with the means of subsistence. In his later writings, Malthus abandoned his pessimistic dogmatism and expressed the hope that man could avoid an application of positive checks through certain *preventive checks*—that is, checks on the birth rate. Malthus proposed late marriage as the best means to reduce the birth rate, since he believed any limitation of births within marriage was immoral.[4]

In the period since the death of Malthus, mankind's situation has been much more fortunate than Malthus envisioned. The positive checks to population growth have not increased their force. On the contrary, death rates today are much lower throughout the world than they were in Malthus's time. Malthus did not foresee the great rise in the means of subsistence which occurred throughout the world after his death, nor did he envision that in many nations birth control within marriage would become an important means of population control.

Nevertheless, the question Malthus raised is no less important today than during his lifetime. The human species in the not-too-distant future *will* experience a rise in its death rate unless the means of subsistence can be increased at the same rate as the population. A rise in mortality can be avoided only through a sizable reduction in the birth rate, a substantial increase in the means of subsistence, or some combination of these two. But none of these more pleasant possibilities is certain to occur.

Harrison Brown, an eminent geochemist, has estimated that with improvements in practice and the development of new technology, world food production can be eventually increased so that it will be sufficient to support 50 billion persons.[5] However, even if we accept the argument

---

3. Thomas Robert Malthus, *Population: The First Essay* (Ann Arbor: Ann Arbor Paperbacks, 1959).

4. Thomas Malthus, "A Summary View of the Principle of Population," in Thomas Malthus et al., *Three Essays on Population* (New York: Mentor Books, 1960), pp. 13–59.

5. Harrison Brown, *The Challenge of Man's Future* (New York: Viking, 1954), pp. 145–48. For a more pessimistic view of this matter see Donella H. Meadows et al., *The Limits to Growth* (New York: Universe Books, 1972).

that eventually the world can support 50 billion persons, we cannot assume that future death rates will not rise. The crucial question is not how many persons can eventually be supported on this planet, but how fast the means of subsistence can be increased. For example, suppose it would take 300 years to increase the means of subsistence sufficiently to support 50 billion persons on earth at the present level of living. Suppose also that population growth continued at its present rate, doubling the population every thirty-five years. Then we would witness the impossible situation of a world population of 50 billion only some 125 years hence, long before the means of subsistence had risen correspondingly. Clearly, if it should take 300 years to increase the means of subsistence sufficient to support 50 billion individuals, then the world rate of population growth cannot continue at its present level but must be reduced in the meantime either by lower fertility or by higher mortality.

In the next two sections of this chapter we will review some of the possibilities of increasing the supply of various resources necessary for human subsistence. It should be emphasized at the outset that this discussion will be in large part speculative, since experts are not always in agreement concerning the feasibility of many of the proposed measures for increasing the supply of these necessities.

Food

Because our knowledge concerning the important question of how rapidly the world's food production can be increased is rather limited, there is great disagreement on the matter among agricultural experts. Statements of opinion tend to shed more heat than light. Arguments over future food availability notwithstanding, much of the world's population is *now* malnourished: millions do not even get enough to eat to prevent gnawing hunger from being an almost constant companion, and many more millions eat a qualitatively inadequate diet in which the principal lack is insufficient protein. In principle, given the proper conditions, the earth's food production could be greatly expanded; but in practice, speaking from an economic and technological point of view, such an expansion could only be undertaken at the cost of massive amounts of money, materials, and energy (all of which those most in need have the least), and even then not to a much greater degree until further advances in technology have been made. In principle, food production can be increased through an *expansion of agriculture acreage,* by means of a *greater yield per acre,* or through *greater exploitation of the oceans.* We shall now discuss each of these three possibilities.

The great increase in world population in the last few centuries was accompanied by a great increase in cropland. In part this was made possible by the continual settlement of many areas, including much of North and South America, Australia, New Zealand, and Siberia, in which agriculture had not previously existed. The increase in cropland also occurred at the expense of forest and pasture land in long-settled agricultural areas. Finally, an increased use of irrigation made agriculture feasible in many arid regions where it had not previously been possible. Can a similar increase in cropland occur in the near future? Several noted experts believe not.[6] Factors that impede the further large-scale expansion of cropland are that much of the present cropland of the world is becoming either severely eroded or waterlogged and is no longer suitable for cultivation and that cropland is also being continuously reduced by urbanization. Moreover, these experts believe that with present technology no new large areas of the world can be opened to agriculture at a feasible cost.

Those agricultural specialists who believe that a large increase in cropland is possible believe that new cropland can be created from the vast tropical rain forests of northern South America, Africa, and Indonesia.[7] These tropic areas, now virtually uninhabited, may contain four-fifths as much potential cropland as the 3.5 billion acres presently cultivated.[8] It should be emphasized, however, that these areas are now unpeopled for the very good reason that with present technology no one can make a living there. These tropic rain-forest areas have the advantages of large amounts of water and sunlight. They have the disadvantages of such poor soil and of being so infested with insects and fungi that all previous attempts at agriculture have failed. Thus, opening these large areas to agriculture, if ever feasible, will first require an intense amount of research to obviate the present obstacles.

The second means of increasing food production that we cited previously is increasing the yield per acre of already cultivated lands. The term *Green Revolution* has been used in reference to certain quite spectacular increases in yield per acre of wheat and rice recently obtained in some of the less developed nations. Before the Green Revolution, yields per acre in these nations were considerably lower than elsewhere.

6. See Lester R. Brown, *Man, Land, and Food* (Washington, D.C.: U.S. Dept. of Agriculture, Economic Research Service, Foreign Regional Analysis Div., 1963); and statement of John J. Haggerty in House Committee on Agriculture, *World War on Hunger*, 89th Congress, 2nd sess., 1966 (Washington, D.C.: Govt. Printing Office, 1966), pp. 68–79.

7. Harrison Brown, *The Challenge of Man's Future* (New York: The Viking Press, 1954), pp. 133–35.

8. Statement of John J. Haggerty, *World War on Hunger*, p. 74.

For example, the rice yields per acre in India were less than one-third as high as those in Japan.[9] Much of the difference in rice yield between India and Japan was caused by special high-yielding strains developed by the Japanese and their use of very large amounts of fertilizer. But an additional factor is that Japan's temperate climate is more favorable to high yields than India's tropical climate, and even with the most advanced farming practices and the best strains, it is not likely that rice yields in India could equal those in Japan.

The essence of the Green Revolution has been the introduction of new strains of wheat and rice suitable for tropical areas which, given an adequate amount of water, ample fertilizer, and, if necessary, insecticides, produce much more heavily than the original strains. For example, the "miracle rice," IR-8, is capable of doubling the yield of most local rices in tropical Asia. The Mexican dwarf wheat developed by Nobel Prize winner Norman Borlaug has had even more remarkable results in those areas to which it is suited; for example, in Mexico wheat yields almost tripled between 1950 and 1965. It must be emphasized however, that very large parts of the Third World have not and cannot profit from the new seeds. In some areas fertilizer may be too expensive, or if applied may simply wash away because the land is too hilly. Furthermore, the Mexican wheats have an advantage over other strains only when they are grown under irrigated or high-rainfall conditions, and the new strains of rice cannot be grown under conditions of natural flooding where they may become submerged.[10]

Insufficient water is therefore a major roadblock to higher yields per crop. Ample water, if made available, would also serve another need. In warm climates a year-round supply of water permits several crops a year rather than the one crop whenever the year is sharply divided into rainy and dry seasons.

In many parts of the world groundwater is pumped from wells and applied to crops either throughout the growing season or for that part of the growing season when rainfall is inadequate. An increasing use of groundwater has been an extremely important component of the increased yields of wheat recently obtained in India and Pakistan.[11] However, groundwater is a capital resource which is not automatically replenished. In many areas the amount of groundwater is steadily declining. For example, in Arizona the groundwater level has receded more than

9. *The State of Food and Agriculture: 1966* (Rome, Italy: Food and Agricultural Organization of the U.N., 1966), p. 140.

10. Lester R. Brown, *Seeds of Change* (New York: Praeger, 1970), pp. 3–43.

11. Ibid., p. 25.

100 feet from its earlier level.[12] Larger pumps may secure greater quantities of water for the near future, but they hasten the time when all groundwater will be exhausted. In areas adjacent to rivers, water for crops may also be made available through construction of reservoirs. But storage of water in reservoirs means that land inundated for the reservoir can no longer be used for production; moreover, a part of the water stored in reservoirs is lost through evaporation. Providing crops with ample water in many arid regions will henceforth require very lengthy transport of water, which will be quite expensive. For example, the Feather River project, which will divert water from northern to southern California, is estimated to cost $2 billion, and its construction to take thirty years.[13]

Desalinization of water is being undertaken in several parts of the world; however, its cost is now so great that it is used only for drinking water and not for agriculture. Even if the price of desalinated water should become much lower, its agricultural use would probably have to be restricted to areas immediately adjacent to a coast, since the cost of transporting it long distances would be very high. The use of water for agriculture must also compete with its use by industry. For example, more than 2,500 tons of water are necessary to manufacture one ton of synthetic rubber.[14] If pollutants can be removed, much of the water used for industrial purposes can be reused for some other purpose. In view of the increased expense in obtaining water, however, we must learn to reuse water much more often than we have in the past.

To some extent, yields per acre can be improved simply through the application of more labor without increasing the supply of other inputs such as water or commercial fertilizer. At least in Indonesian rice paddies, it would appear that total production can be almost indefinitely increased through additions to the number of cultivators.[15]

Finally, yields of food per acre can be improved considerably if men can learn to live without protein from animal sources. From five to eight calories of food from plants are needed to produce each calorie of foodstuff obtained by humans from animals.[16] Thus, food from animal sources is extremely wasteful of plant calories, and this is a chief reason

12. Georg Borgstrom, *The Hungry Planet* (New York: Macmillan, 1965), p. 417.

13. Ibid., p. 425.

14. Ibid., p. 423.

15. Clifford Geertz, *Agricultural Involution* (Berkeley, Calif.: University of California Press, 1963), p. 32.

16. Borgstrom, *The Hungry Planet*, p. 28.

why in many Asian nations very little food comes from such sources. At present a very large proportion of mankind suffers from a protein deficiency. If men could get the right kind of protein exclusively from plants, they could obtain more calories for themselves because of feeding fewer animals, and they might also obtain more much-needed protein for themselves. Recently a packaged combination of different vegetable products, including an oil-seed meal and a cereal which together create a balanced protein product, has been developed and marketed under the name of *Incaparina*.[17] Wider distribution of this product holds great promise. Another means of obtaining inexpensive protein may be the development of yeast factories. Yeast, a source of high protein, can be grown with great efficiency from sugar cane.[18] Algae may be yet another future source of high-quality protein, but the intensive cultivation of algae would demand the expenditure of very large amounts of capital, and the cost of maintaining production might be either high or low.[19]

Man may also be able to increase the amount of food gathered from the sea. In fact, since the end of World War II the production of food from marine sources has increased more rapidly than that from terrestrial sources.[20] Much of this increase in fisheries production came about from stepped-up fishing activity in the Southern Hemisphere, particularly off the coast of Peru. It is believed that we are currently fully exploiting or even overexploiting the fish from the North Atlantic Ocean, but that further increases in catch can be obtained from oceans in the Southern Hemisphere, particularly the Indian Ocean.[21] Incidentally, a promising new product from the new fishing grounds off the coast of Peru is fish protein concentrate. This fish flour, obtained from grinding whole fish, is now largely used as feed for poultry and livestock but can be used to provide valuable and inexpensive protein to human beings as well.

The problem of increasing world food production is made much more difficult because the greatest need for increased production is in the rapidly growing economically backward nations where the obstacles to securing a sufficient food production increase appear to be greatest.

---

17. Nevin S. Scrimshaw, "Adapting Food Supplies and Processing Methods to Fit Nutritional Needs," in *World Population and Food Supplies, 1980*, ASA Special Publication No. 6 (Madison, Wis.: American Society of Agronomy, 1965), pp. 31–41.

18. Ibid., p. 39.

19. Ibid.

20. *The State of Food and Agriculture: 1971* (Rome, Italy: Food and Agricultural Organization of the U.N., 1971), p.1.

21. S. J. Holt, "The Food Resources of hte Ocean," *Scientific American* (September 1969), 221:3, pp. 178–94.

We cannot be sure that the less developed nations will be able to increase their food production sufficiently to keep up with their increase in population. If they do not, and if the United States and others of the food-surplus nations can no longer meet the food deficits of these nations, death rates in the latter will surely rise. It is clear, however, that by providing extensive technical and scientific assistance, the developed countries can greatly help the less developed nations increase their food supplies.

Energy and Minerals

The future demand for energy and minerals will be increased not only by population growth but also by economic development. The world's population is now doubling approximately every thirty-five years. But the world consumption of energy has been growing at a rate which ensures a doubling of consumption approximately every twelve years, and production of iron ore at a rate which ensures doubling approximately every eleven years.[22] In the early 1960s over 92 percent of the world's energy consumption was derived from fossil fuel resources (i.e., from coal, petroleum, and natural gas), and less than 8 percent from the generation of hydroelectric power, atomic energy, or other means.[23] Nevertheless, in the face of a very rapid increase in energy consumption, mankind will soon be confronted with the exhaustion of its supply of energy from fossil fuels.

The United States is extremely favored in its reserves of fossil fuels. Yet in 1954 Harrison Brown estimated that the fossil fuel resources in the United States might last no longer than 75 years, or at most no longer than 250 years.[24] Estimates of when the world's fossil fuels will be exhausted are of course subject to considerable error, since we do not have accurate knowledge of what or where all reserves actually exist, especially with regard to petroleum and natural gas, nor can we predict how fast the demand for fossil fuels will grow in the near future. Nevertheless, it is clear that the era of fossil fuel consumption will be but a very short time period in the total span of human history. Recent events

22. Approximate doubling times were computed from data in United Nations, *Statistical Yearbook, 1965* (New York: United Nations, 1966), pp. 347 and 186.

23. Sir Harold Hartley, "World Energy Prospects," in *The World in 1984*, Vol. I, ed. Nigel Calder (Baltimore: Penguin Books, 1965), p. 71.

24. Harrison Brown, *The Challenge of Man's Future* (New York: Viking Press, 1954), p. 164. For another similar estimate, see Richard L. Meier, *Science and Economic Development: New Patterns of Living* (Cambridge, Mass.: The MIT Press, 1966), p. 29.

make it apparent that unless energy can be produced from other sources as cheaply as from fossil fuels, the world will have to get along with less energy or pay more for what it gets.

Further development of water power will provide some small relief when fossil fuels have been exhausted. However, we must expect that in the future the major sources of energy will come from atomic power and perhaps from the direct tapping of solar energy. If nuclear fission becomes the major source of the world's energy, the supply of high-grade uranium and thorium ores will eventually be exhausted. However, if all the uranium and thorium within one ton of ordinary rock could be utilized for energy release, energy equivalent to that within fifty tons of coal could be obtained.[25] Thus, in principle man could use ordinary rock for his fuel-energy needs.

Because future technological developments cannot be predicted in advance, we cannot forecast in detail the future cost of energy. In some areas and for certain purposes, atomic energy is now the least expensive energy source; operating costs at nuclear power plants are now relatively low. The major reason why atomic energy is not now usually competitive with fossil fuels is the high cost of the interest payments on the enormous uranium or thorium inventory which is currently necessary for nuclear energy production. A major reduction in the cost of atomic power will result when and if a safe and environmentally harmless breeder reactor is developed. Current nuclear reactors are capable of utilizing only uranium-235, which makes up only 1.5 percent of the fission energy contained in uranium, and cannot utilize the very much more common uranium-238. The breeder reactors will allow fission of uranium-238 and will produce perhaps fifty times as much energy from a given amount of uranium as is obtainable by current methods. The United States government has announced a national policy of hastening the development of the breeder reactor. Conversely, unless a safe and effective breeder reactor can be developed quickly, an acute shortage of uranium ores is likely to develop before the end of the century which would cause the cost of atomic power to rise substantially.[26]

The future cost of metals will also be greatly affected by the future costs of energy. All nations are exhausting their supplies of high-grade iron ore and the other high-grade metallic ores necessary for modern industry. For example, the United States is increasingly mining taconite,

25. Brown, *The Challenge of Man's Future*, p. 174.

26. See "Energy" in Roger Revelle et al., eds., *The Survival Equation* (Boston, Mass.: Houghton Mifflin, 1971), pp. 208–17; Chauncey Starr, "Energy and Power," *Scientific American* (September 1971), 225:3, pp. 37–49; and M. King Hubbert, "The Energy Resources of the Earth," *Scientific American* (September 1971), 225:3, pp. 61–70.

a relatively low-grade iron ore. Obtaining metal from low-grade rather than high-grade ores requires a much greater expenditure of energy. Thus, the cost of metals will be much affected in the future by the costs of energy production.

LIFE IN A MORE CROWDED WORLD

Although demographers may disagree on how fast the world's population will grow and when the human population will reach its peak, almost all of them would agree that the world's population will probably be considerably more dense in coming years than it has been in the past. Assuming that present standards of living throughout the world will at least be maintained and that death rates will not rise, what will be some of the other consequences of life in a more crowded world?

Perhaps one of the most important consequences will be the emergence of tighter social controls on certain activities. For example, a very large increase in the amount of vehicular traffic will necessitate more complex traffic rules. Traffic may become so dense that human beings may have to abdicate the management of their automobiles to computers. Controls over water and air pollution will also have to become more strict. As populations increase, the efficiency with which water is used and reused will have to increase greatly. Industrial plants which place large quantities of pollutants into water will have to be zoned into areas so that they are the last users of water. As the number of large cities grow, air pollution will tend to become much more intense. Each city will find that more and more of its air has been polluted from emissions rising over other cities. Hence, national and even international controls over air pollution will become necessary. Since a constantly expanding population may seem undesirable, many nations may attempt to reduce the fertility of their populations through such measures as monetary rewards for bearing fewer children or for having oneself sterilized.

A direct result of crowding will be that the amount of space per capita will decrease. This will have immediate consequences even in the United States, where general living space is still ample, although even now the country suffers from overcrowding in its places of prime scenic and historic interest. In recent years the number of persons visiting areas of scenic or historic interest in our national park system has been more than 200 million a year, approximately twenty times the annual number of visitors in the 1930s.[27] If our population continues to increase,

27. U.S. Bureau of the Census, *Statistical Abstract of the United States, 1965* (Washington, D.C.: Government Printing Office, 1965), p. 201 and U.S. Bureau of the Census, *Statistical Abstract of the United States, 1972* (Washington, D.C.: Government Printing Office, 1972), p. 201.

we may have to prohibit visits to such places except on the basis of reservations made long in advance.

Environmental mastery in a more crowded world will depend on man's ability to make changes continually in his relation to his environment. Many well-intentioned changes actually prove to be harmful: because ecological chains are so complicated, each environmental change is subject to the possibility of unintended consequences. A familiar recent example of unintended consequences resulting from attempts at environmental change is the reduction of many bird populations following the attempt to kill harmful insects with DDT, dieldrin, and other powerful insecticides. Systems research, using high-speed computers, may help to prevent reoccurrences of such ecological errors, but it is doubtful that we will ever be able to avoid completely all the possible harmful consequences of environmental change.

CHAPTER 3
THE GEOGRAPHIC DISTRIBUTION OF POPULATION

THE GENERAL DISTRIBUTION OF THE WORLD'S POPULATION

In spite of man's flexibility in adapting to a large number of different environments, human beings have found certain environments much more congenial than others. As a result, vast areas of land have either a scanty population or none at all. Antarctica is perhaps the most conspicuous example of a large land area which has no permanent human inhabitants. As figure 1 shows, other sparsely populated areas of the world are found in the arctic zones of North America and Asia, the vast desert region extending from Northern Africa through central Asia, the arid interior of Australia, the mountainous areas in North and South America and Africa, and elsewhere. The world distribution of population is so uneven that nearly half of the world's population lives on 5 percent of this planet's total land area.[1]

The distribution of the world's population can best be explained through two frames of reference, or "frameworks," one environmental and the other historical. If one were interested in an ideal distribution of population, one would have to pay attention only to environmental factors, but the human population on earth is not ideally located (no matter how the ideals might be defined), and the actual distribution of population on earth is as much affected by historical as by environmental factors.

1. United Nations, *Determinants and Consequences of Population Trends* (New York: United Nations, 1953), p. 163.

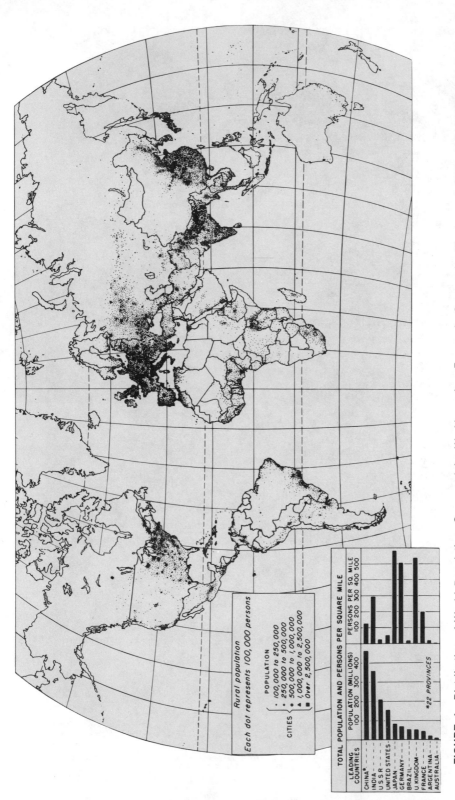

FIGURE 1 Distribution of World Population. Source: John W. Alexander, *Economic Geography* (Englewood Cliffs, N.J.: Prentice-Hall, Inc., 1963).

The environmental factors affecting population distribution at a given point in time are: (1) *climate*, (2) *location of water, soil, energy, and mineral resources*, and (3) *transport relationships*.

Climate bears some rather obvious relationships to population distribution. Large parts of the world attract either no people at all or at best only a few hardy or adventurous ones because of the temperature. Man can, of course, live in almost any environment having an unfavorable temperature, but he finds other environments less costly, both monetarily and energy-wise. Very cold climates present extreme obstacles to human habitation: they are very unfavorable for food production, and clothing and shelter must be more elaborate. At present the very cold climates are inhabited only where they contain valuable minerals or where the area is strategic for military or scientific reasons. The hot tropic areas of the world are much more densely populated than the polar areas. However, the tropics also present some difficulties for human habitation: tropic environment causes a higher incidence of infectious disease, mainly because there is no seasonal check on (that is, no cold-weather hiatus for) the insect, bacterial, and fungus populations; and a combination of high heat and humidity, unless artificially altered through air conditioning, reduces human work efficiency.

Large groups of people need very large quantities of water at cheap cost, since an ample supply of water is necessary not only for direct use as drinking water and for cleanliness, but also for agriculture and manufacturing. Human population is dense mostly in areas where the rainfall is adequate. If rainfall is deficient, a dense population can be maintained only if there is abundant groundwater, a large nearby river, facilities for transporting water inexpensively by pipeline or aqueduct, or processing plants for the inexpensive desalinization of seawater.

The quality of soil under cultivated use is also an important determinant of population distribution. The three best soils are (1) alluvial deposits in river valleys, (2) volcanic soils, and (3) the chernozem (black earth) soils of certain temperate grasslands. Soils such as these are capable of producing large quantities of food per acre and hence can support quite dense populations. The soils of poorest quality are the latosols (leached red and yellow), covering much of tropic Africa and Latin America, and the podzolic (organic/mineral—ashy) soils of the arctic and subarctic regions. In their areas, population is usually very slight. The absence of soil, as in mountainous regions of rock surface, is an even more severe inhibitor of high population density.

A mineral or energy resource may also attract population. If such resources are to be exploited, the population must be at least large enough to provide the labor force necessary for mining or extraction. If the resource is very bulky, additional population may locate near it because it is often more profitable to use the resource where it is taken from the earth than elsewhere. Iron and steel industries thus, often tend to locate near coal mines because a large amount of coal is used in manufacturing iron and steel. In turn, an area with a large iron and steel industry tends to attract so many manufacturers of fabricated metal products that a coal-mining area often becomes a major center of heavy industry.

The third environmental determinant of population distribution is transport relationships. Since almost all of the resources for human subsistence can be used at some site other than that in which they are found naturally, certain areas may become important centers of population if their costs of transport from resource areas to market areas are low. With present technology, cost of water transport is usually much cheaper than transportation by land. Hence, coastal areas and islands are apt to be areas which can cheaply assemble raw materials from elsewhere, process them, and ship the finished product to other markets. England exemplifies an area with very favorable transport relationships. The density of population in other nations is hampered by poor transport relationships. Countries with a rugged terrain, such as Mexico and Colombia, have poor transport relationships because the costs of highway and railroad construction are so high. Similarly, transport relationships are poor in land-locked nations situated at great distances from markets or resource areas.

If the population of the world were able to be redistributed to maximize human comforts, environmental factors would be the sole basis for redistribution. However, since this population apparently has not been distributed with its own comfort in mind, the explanation for the existing population distribution must then depend on various historical factors, such as *past demographic trends, environmental advantages,* and *social policies.*

Demographic trends undoubtedly have had a crucial influence on the present distribution of the earth's population. The United States, for example, possesses a very large share of the total natural resources of the world, but only a small share of its population. Before the sixteenth century, the area which is now the United States was populated by tribes with such a low level of technology that their population density was very slight; since that century, despite a very rapid growth in population, the United States has not had time to develop a very dense population. Hence the amount of natural resources per capita of total population in the United States remains extremely high relative to that of almost all of the remainder of the world. By contrast, China, India, Pakistan, Indonesia, and many other nations have had a positive growth rate for such a long period of time that resources per capita have become extremely limited.

Actually, once it has had the effect of drawing enough people to its locus, an environmental advantage is never exhausted—not even if drastic changes are made in the original surroundings. It is never exhausted because it helps to determine the density of all future populations: once an area becomes densely populated, it achieves and stands a good chance to retain a transport advantage over more thinly populated competitive regions in marketing its produce, and this factor alone will continue to attract people. Proof of the thesis that environmental advantage is never exhausted may be seen in the present concentration of population on the northeast coast of the United States (which, however, might not prove to be the most popular distribution area if the United States were suddenly depopulated and could be populated again). The existing high density of population in this section of the nation is at least partly because it was the closest to Europe, and it gained a transportation advantage by attracting both the bulk of the first European settlers and the lion's share of the early market-produce business.

New York may be America's largest city as a result of its past environmental advantages. New York's port does not now have any noticeable intrinsic advantage over those in Norfolk, Baltimore, or Philadelphia; all of these are closer to America's heartland. What gave New York its greatest advantage over its competitors was the building of the Erie Canal, completed in 1825. Upon the canal's opening, the freight rate from Buffalo to New York declined from $100 to $10 a ton, and travel time from fifteen to six days.[2] As a result, the population of New York City soon outstripped that of its principal rivals (Baltimore, Philadelphia, and Boston) which, without canals, did not have cheap access to the interior. Today railroads and highways are New York's chief links to the hinterlands, and New York no longer has a transport advantage in obtaining goods from inland America. Because of the great lead in population which she attained as a result of the Erie Canal, however, New York has been able to maintain its position as the largest city in the United States.

The third historical factor influencing population distribution is social policy. Because dense populations tend to maintain themselves, past social policies that helped to determine these densities are important in explaining current population densities. For example, although Brazilia has recently been made the capital of Brazil, Rio de Janeiro the previous seat of government, had in 1970 a population of 4.3 million, in contrast to less than 3 hundred thousand in Brazilia, mainly because it was Brazil's capital for so many years. Beside the choice of the capital city, other social policies which can also determine population distribu-

2. *Encyclopaedia Britannica*, 1965, s.v. "Erie Canal."

tion within a nation may be found in current and past legislation concerning tariffs, agricultural subsidies, migration, and area development. The current population distribution among nations is also influenced by such past and present social policies as warfare and restrictions on international migration.

Changes in population distribution result from several factors. In the very long run, they may be due to environmental changes, but environmental changes usually occur very slowly and hence are quite unimportant to short-run changes in population distribution. Changes in technology, in population growth rates, and in social policy are probably the most important determinants of short-term shifts in population distribution.

URBANIZATION

In many nations one of the most striking characteristics of the last 200 years has been the tremendous change in the proportion of population living in cities—a change termed *urbanization*. Kingsley Davis has estimated that the proportion of the total world population living in urban areas of 100,000 population or more increased from around 2 percent in 1800 to about 18 percent in 1960.[3] Urbanization has been closely associated with economic development. In the history of the now developed nations, each increase in material well-being was associated with a greater proportion of the total population living in urban areas. For example, in the United States the proportion of all population classified as urban residents increased from 5.1 percent in 1790 to 73.5 percent in 1970.[4] Currently, the most economically developed nations are also for the most part the most urbanized, and the least developed the least urbanized. For example, in the United States, the world's most wealthy nation, 55.5 percent of the population lived in urbanized areas of more than 100,000 population in 1970,[5] while in India, one of the world's poorest nations, only 8 percent of the population lived in urban areas of this size class in 1964.[6]

The urbanization of the world during the last 200 years has had

3. Kingsley Davis, "The Urbanization of the Human Population," *Scientific American* (September, 1965), 233:3, 44.

4. U.S. Bureau of the Census, *United States Census of Population: 1970*, Final Report PC(1)-A1, p. 42.

5. Ibid., p. 43.

6. United Nations, *Demographic Yearbook, 1964* (New York: United Nations, 1965), pp. 178–79.

two fundamental causes. First, as a nation becomes more wealthy, its inhabitants desire to spend less of their income on food and more on other goods and services. Consumer goods other than food are almost invariably produced more cheaply in cities than in the countryside, because cities are centers of transportation and thus can assemble raw materials and ship out a finished product at a relatively low cost, and also because cities can provide a labor force sufficient to produce commodities by mass production—a method which in most cases results in cheaper costs all around. Cities are also the best locations for many specialized services. If, for example, a medical specialist were to locate in the middle of the countryside, he would have a hard time making a living because he would see so few patients; if, however, he located in a city, he would have patients not only from that city but also from many outlying areas to which the city is linked by its transportation network. Thus such specialized services as wholesale trade, higher education, hospital services, banking, and insurance are almost invariably located in urban areas. Because cities can provide many services which rural areas cannot, they often attract people who might have equal or better economic opportunity elsewhere. In such cases, the urban economic opportunity stimulates urbanization, and urbanization in turn stimulates the economic opportunity available in cities.

The second major reason for urbanization has been the changing character of food production. Before the scientific-industrial revolution the number of input goods necessary to achieve the production of agricultural products was very few, and the input goods used were usually produced by the farmer himself. Today, at least in the developed nations, the situation is very different. To create their produce, farmers increasingly rely on artificial fertilizers, insecticides, machinery, and inanimate sources of energy. These many inputs to agricultural production cannot be produced directly on the farm but instead are usually produced in urban centers. As a result, a large part of "farm" work is now done not on the farm but in cities. Furthermore, for the many persons in the developed nations who do not themselves live on farms, food which remains on the farm is of no direct use. To be useful to urbanites, farm produce must be transported from the farm, processed, and then distributed, and these additional activities are commonly carried out by persons who themselves dwell in cities. Hence for any typical food product, the farmer receives only a very small share of the total price. For example, in the United States in 1966 a quart of milk cost the consumer 28¢, while the farmer received only 2.8¢ for it.[7]

Concomitant with increasing urbanization in the developed nations

7. Robert E. Dallos, "Milk: Case History of a Rising Price," *New York Times,* 7 August 1966.

has been a phenomenon which I shall call *suburbanization*. "Suburbanization" can mean several things, though perhaps its most common meaning would be "an increase in the proportion of the total population in a metropolis which lives outside the official limits of the central city of that metropolis." In the United States and other developed nations there has certainly been a much more rapid growth in the political areas of the metropolis outside the central city than within its bounds. However, the suburbanization to which I wish to refer can occur *both* in the central city *and* in surrounding adjacent cities and towns. What I wish to discuss is a tendency for the parts of the metropolis nearest the central business district to decline in population while those most removed from the central business district increase dramatically.

Suburbanization has been perhaps most pronounced in the United States, but the phenomenon exists in all developed nations. The process of suburbanization can be well illustrated by the example of the New York urbanized area during the period from 1950 to 1970. During those years the total population of the New York-northeastern New Jersey urbanized area increased from 12.3 million to 16.2 million persons. The urbanized land area however, increased even more than the population per square mile so that the population per square mile for the whole urbanized land area declined from 9,810 to 6,683. In Manhattan, the center of the urbanized area, the population declined from 89,000 persons per square mile to 69,000. Consider now the pattern of population density to the east of Manhattan. Brooklyn and the Bronx, densely settled boroughs immediately adjacent to Manhattan on the southeast and northeast respectively, experienced little change in population density. In Brooklyn the decline in population was from 36,000 persons per square mile to 34,000; in the Bronx, density remained constant at 34,000 persons per square mile. Queens Borough, somewhat farther east from Manhattan than Brooklyn or the Bronx, had a slight gain in population from 14,000 to 17,000 persons per square mile, whereas Nassau County, on Long Island immediately east of Queens Borough and outside the limits of New York City, more than doubled its population from 2,200 persons per square mile to 4,700. Simultaneously, Suffolk County, located to the east of Nassau County, experienced a phenomenal rise in density from 300 persons per square mile to 1,200.[8]

Suburbanization has several causes. One is that residential use of land must compete with other land uses. Increasingly, land adjacent to the central business district is taken over for expressways, parking lots, and commercial use, and as a result, residential density declines.

8.   U.S. Bureau of the Census, *United States Census of Population, 1960*, Vol. 1, Part 1, p. 45; and Vol. 1, Part 34, p. 13; and U.S. Bureau of the Census, *U.S. Census of Population: 1970*, Final Report PC(1)-A34, p. 21.

A second cause involves changes in the demand for residential space brought about by changes in income, the number of leisure hours, and the cost of travel. Larger incomes have allowed larger proportions of more salaries to be spent on travel to and from work, and shorter work-days have given the commuter more time for such travel. In addition, the automobile has greatly reduced the cost and time of commuting between the central city and suburban areas, some remote enough not to be linked to the central city by public transport. Further, families have moved out of the areas adjacent to the central business districts to escape high land costs, soaring rents, and a general lack of elbowroom.

Thirdly, with an increasing volume of goods shipped by truck rather than by railroad, and with a rising proportion of workers commuting by automobile rather than by public transportation, it has also been possible for a larger proportion of factories to locate away from the central business area. An increasing dispersion of jobs also reinforces a dispersion of residence.

A fourth cause for suburbanization relates to the quality of existing city housing and the phenomenon of rising per-capita income. In the areas adjacent to the central business district, housing is generally rather crowded. As the average income of the population of the inner-city area increases, the residents wish to spend more money on housing. The usual pattern is one of demanding more space per capita. Hence, dwelling units are remodeled, and a house which originally was built for two families is converted to a single-family house. In Boston, which lost about 20 percent of its population from 1950 to 1970 the proportion of housing units with more than one person per room declined from 12.7 percent to 7.6 percent.[9] Similar declines in crowding within housing units have occurred in Manhattan and in the East Side of London, two areas which have also declined in total population.[10]

SOCIAL EFFECTS OF HIGH
AND LOW POPULATION DENSITY

Before we study the effects of differences in population density, we must define the term. The most common definition of *population density,*

---

9. U.S. Bureau of the Census, *United States Census of Population, 1950*, Vol. 3, Chapter 6, p. 86; and U.S. Bureau of the Census, *U.S. Census of Population and Housing: 1970*, Final Report PHC(1)-29, p. P-3 and p. H-3.

10. U.S. Bureau of the Census, *United States Census of Housing, 1950*, Vol. 1, Part 4, P. 32–29; U.S. Bureau of the Census, *U.S. Census of Housing: 1970*, Final Report HC(1)-A34, p. 44; and Peter Hall, *The World Cities* (New York: McGraw-Hill, 1966), pp. 38–44.

as it applies to a given place, is "the number of persons per unit of area in that place." A difficulty with the population per areal unit is that the density we compute is only for the place itself and does not take into account the density of contiguous areas.

A second definition of population density for a given place might be "the number of persons per unit of housing space in that place." Such a definition is very different from the first. Thus in impoverished rural areas the amount of living space per capita may be very small, but the distance between dwellings very large. Moreover, an area containing high-rise luxury apartments would have a low density according to this definition, whereas according to the first definition its density would be very high. Furthermore, the social effects also appear to vary depending on the definition. For example, a recent study of local areas within Chicago revealed that the number of persons per housing unit *was* associated with various pathologies, whereas persons per unit of area was not.[11]

A third definition of population density has been termed *population potential*. Although the concept of population potential is somewhat harder to comprehend than the two preceding definitions of population density, it is for many purposes the most useful of the possible definitions. *Therefore, in future references to population density, we shall take it to refer to population potential.* Population potential measures not only the population per area at a particular location, but also the number of persons who are contiguous to that location. Making use of population-distance ratios, it is computed for a given reference point by dividing the total population at each separate point in the nation (or other unit) by the distance of that point from the reference point, and then summing these population-distance ratios over all points in the nation (or other areal unit). Stated in mathematical notation, the definition of population potential is as follows:

$$\text{Population potential at reference point} = \sum_{i=1}^{k} \frac{\text{Population at point } i}{\text{Distance of point } i \text{ from the reference point}}$$

In the United States the point of highest population potential is New York City; the central districts of all other large urban areas also have high population potential. In rural parts of the United States a belt of relatively high population potential covers the whole area from

---

11. Omer R. Galle, Walter R. Gove, and J. M. McPherson, "Population Density and Pathology: What are the Relationships for Man?" *Science* (7 April 1972), 176, 23–30.

Boston to Norfolk on the East and from St. Louis to Milwaukee on the West.[12]

Assuming that population potential is the most satisfactory way to define population density, we will still have difficulty in ascertaining its social effects, since there are many problems in separating the effects of population density from the effects of the many other variables that are commonly associated with it. For example, if we wish to examine the differential effects of the high population potential characteristic of central cities in the United States from the lower population potential of their suburbs, we should have to separate the effects of such facts as these: (1) central cities tend to have older, more crowded housing than their suburbs; (2) central cities tend to contain higher proportions of lower socio-economic groups and of blacks, the foreign-born, and persons not living in family units; (3) central cities may or may not contain a higher proportion of new arrivals than their suburbs.

As a result of these difficulties in disentangling the effect of other variables, our empirical knowledge of the social effects of population density is still rather slight. It may therefore help our understanding of the effects of differences in population density if we consider two sets of deductive arguments in connection with the empirical knowledge that is available. First of all, when population density is high, an individual is in close physical contact with many more persons than when it is low. It is then likely that both the total number of persons with whom he will have social contact and the range in types of persons will vary directly with the population density. Secondly, human beings are biologically limited both in the number of persons with whom they can be acquainted and in the number they can know well. Therefore, a higher proportion of all social contacts in the area of high population density might be expected to be superficial or secondary relationships which are functionally specific and affectively neutral, whereas a high proportion of all contacts where population density is low would be primary relationships, functionally more diffuse and expressive of stronger emotions.

From these considerations it is plausible to argue that very low or very high population densities are inimical to human welfare. A very low population density, though sought and appreciated by a few, for the vast majority leads to loneliness occasioned not only by the absolute paucity of other human contacts but by the fact that the types of persons who may be most congenial to a given individual may be altogether lacking in the restricted circle of possible acquaintances. It may also lead to the inability to procure many necessary services, except at prohibitive

---

12. For a further discussion of population potential, see Otis Dudley Duncan et al., *Statistical Geography* (Glencoe, Ill.: The Free Press, 1961), pp. 52–55.

costs of transportation and may restrict the flow of new and useful ideas. High population density, on the other hand, will at least allow the individual an opportunity to form congenial associations with the like-minded. It will also allow him to procure many specialized services and will foster the spread of new and useful ideas. However, the sheer number of social contacts which high population density forces on one may cause mental stress to develop, of a type and intensity which may be clearly exemplified by the strain one encounters in driving in the midst of a rush-hour traffic jam.

Some interesting experiments by John B. Calhoun on populations of laboratory rats illustrate the pathology which can be created by the mental stress occasioned by extreme population densities.[13] In Calhoun's experiments, all of the rat populations were supplied with an abundance of food and were free from the attacks of predators. However, under conditions of high population density, mother rats failed to build nests or to nurse their young adequately. As a result, infant mortality among the high-density rats was very high. Maternal mortality also rose with increased population density. Many male rats developed various disorders, including homosexuality, extreme aggression, cannibalism of infant rats, and a very obvious desire for isolation.

The mental stress and even loneliness of life for humans living in areas of high population density has been stressed by Louis Wirth.[14] Wirth argued that the excessive number of superficial contacts made necessary in a situation of high population density reduces the possibility of primary relationships and contended that life in the big city is essentially lonely. However, more recent data suggest that Wirth's view of the loneliness of big-city life exaggerates the extent to which primary contacts are lacking in areas of high population density. William Foote Whyte's *Street Corner Society* showed the existence of very strong primary ties among the young men living in the North End of Boston, an Italian working-class district of high population density.[15] Similarly, Young and Willmott's *Family and Kinship in East London* reported extensive primary relationships in that dense working-class area.[16] In fact, Young and

13. John B. Calhoun, "Population Density and Social Pathology," *Scientific American* (February, 1962), 206:2, 139–48.

14. Louis Wirth, "Urbanism as a Way of Life," *American Journal of Sociology* (July, 1938), 44:1, 1–24.

15. William Foote Whyte, *Street Corner Society* (Chicago, Ill.: University of Chicago Press, 1943).

16. Michael Young and Peter Willmott, *Family and Kinship in East London* (London; Routledge & Kegan Paul, 1957).

Willmott found primary relationships to be considerably stronger in Bethnal Green, their study area in London's East End, than in Greenleigh, their suburban study area, a "new town" situated some twenty miles away from downtown London.

It should be noted that the high-density areas studied by Whyte and by Young and Willmott were both areas of stable and homogeneous population. It is likely that high population density has relatively little harmful effect in such conditions, whereas it may become distinctly harmful if it occurs in conjunction with a heterogeneous population containing many recent arrivals. The murder of Catherine Genovese which occurred in 1964 in Queens Borough, New York, may illustrate the type of social pathology occasioned by high population density in conjunction with these other conditions. Miss Genovese was stabbed in three separate attacks and finally killed by her assailant, while none of the thirty-eight neighbors who witnessed the attack attempted to discourage her assailant or *even to notify the police*. The incident fostered great anxiety among opinion leaders in the United States concerning the adequacy of primary social controls in densely populated urban areas.[17]

We shall discuss more thoroughly, in the chapter on migration, the consequences to an already populous area of a high proportion of recent arrivals. In concluding this discussion of the social effects of differences in population density, it would be well to repeat that this topic, although as yet inadequately studied, is one of great significance.

17. *The New York Times*, 27 March 1964, p. 1; 28 March 1964 (editorial), pp. 18 and 28; and 3 May 1964, Sec. 6, p. 24.

PART TWO
POPULATION PROCESSES

CHAPTER 4
MORTALITY

MEASUREMENT OF MORTALITY

The *crude death-rate* is perhaps the most commonly used measure of mortality. It may be defined as "the ratio of the number of deaths which occur within a given population during a specified year to the size of that population at midyear." Frequently, however, the crude death-rate does not provide a very accurate indicator of mortality conditions, since it is very much affected by age structure. A young population will always have a lower crude death-rate than an older population, even though the death rates at each age in the two populations are identical. Furthermore, differences between two populations in their sex ratio will also affect the crude death-rate, since at each age, death rates for females are usually somewhat lower than for males.

An exact comparison of mortality in two different populations can be made by a separate presentation of the death rates in each age-sex group of each population. This method is illustrated in Table 3, which presents male age-specific death rates for the United States and for Peru in 1961. Table 3 shows clearly that at each age, mortality is distinctly higher for males in Peru than for males in the United States. The table also demonstrates the very great differences in mortality by age within each of these two populations. For both nations the death rates by age form roughly a U-shaped distribution. Death rates are relatively high in the first year of life, rapidly decline in early childhood, reach their minimum around ages 10 to 14, and then rise gradually but steadily until they reach their maximum at old age.

Table 3   Male Age-Specific Death Rates for the United States and for Peru, 1961 (per 1,000 population)

AGE	U.S.	PERU
0	29.2	176.3
1–4	1.1	17.0
5–9	0.5	7.0
10–14	0.5	2.5
15–19	1.2	4.5
20–24	1.7	6.3
25–29	1.7	7.0
30–34	2.0	7.4
35–39	2.8	8.4
40–44	4.5	10.4
45–49	7.3	13.6
50–54	12.4	18.4
55–59	17.9	25.2
60–64	27.9	35.8
65–69	41.4	53.0
70–74	57.4	76.3
75–79	83.4	114.9
80–84	128.3	190.6
85 and over	219.6	278.7

Source: U.S. Dept. of Health, Education, and Welfare, "Life Tables," in *Vital Statistics of the United States, 1961*, Vol. 2, Sec. 2, p. 7; and Eduardo E. Arriaga, "New Abridged Life Tables for Peru: 1940, 1950–51, and 1961," *Demography* (1966), 3:1, 226.

Life tables provide the most complete picture of mortality in a given population. Two types of table can be constructed, the most common of which, termed a *period* life table, summarizes the age-sex-specific mortality conditions pertaining in a given year or other short time-period. The second type of life table, called a *cohort* or *generation* life table, summarizes the age-sex-specific mortality experience of a given birth cohort (a group of persons born at the same time) for its lifetime, and thus extends over many calendar years.

Both types of life table assume a cohort of fixed size at birth—usually 100,000—and provide the following data for each year of age: (1) the probability of death during the year for those persons entering an exact age x (q_x); (2) the number of deaths occurring between exact age x and exact age $x + 1$ (d_x); (3) the number of survivors to exact age x (l_x); (4) the number of years of life lived by the cohort between exact age x and age $x + 1$ (L_x); (5) the total years of life lived by the cohort from age x to the end of the human lifespan (T_x); and (6) the mean number of years of life remaining from age x to the end of the lifespan (e°_x).

A variant of the complete life table, which provides mortality data for each single year of age, is the abridged life table, which provides data for persons in age-groups, usually of five-year intervals. An abridged life table for United States males in 1969 is presented in Table 4. In this table the prefix n refers to the number of years in the age interval. Thus $_nL_x$ denotes the number of years of life lived between age x and age $x + n$.

Perhaps the most commonly used datum from the life table is the *average* or *mean expectation of life at birth* (e^o_0). A principal advantage of the mean expectation of life at birth as a summary measure of mortality is that, unlike the crude death-rate, it does not depend on the age structure of the population.

Two additional summary measures of mortality are also free of distortion due to differences in age composition. One of these is termed an *age-standardized* or *age-adjusted death rate*. This is obtained by computing for each age-sex group the product of its specific death-rate and a fraction equal to the proportion belonging to that particular age-sex group in a "standard" population and then summing these products over every age-group and each sex. Mortality in various populations may be easily compared when the same standard population is used to "weight" the age-sex-specific mortality rates in each population. Another summary measure of mortality in frequent use is the *standard mortality ratio,* which equals 100 times the ratio of the actual crude death-rate in a population to the rate which would have been expected if for each age-sex group in the actual population the death rate were identical to that in some "standard" population. Mortality in various populations can again be easily compared when standard mortality ratios are computed for several populations, in every case using the same set of rates as the standard in constructing the "expected" death rate.

Mortality Differentials

In the previous section we discussed how mortality rates vary by age and sex, and what methods are available for comparing mortality after making allowances for differences between populations in their age-sex composition. We are now in a position to discuss some other types of mortality differentials. Some of the mortality differences of prime interest to sociologists are those discriminating between: (1) times of peace and war, (2) different social classes within a nation, (3) developed and less-developed nations, and (4) current national levels compared to previous levels in those nations. Let us discuss each of these four differentials in turn.

Wars may or may not have a major effect on a nation's mortality.

Table 4   Abridged Life Table for the Male Population: United States, 1969

	AGE INTERVAL	PROPORTION DYING	OF 100,000 BORN ALIVE		STATIONARY POPULATION		AVERAGE REMAINING LIFETIME
	Period of life between two exact ages stated in years x to $x + n$	Proportion of persons alive at beginning of age interval dying during interval $q_{n\,x}$	Number living at beginning of age interval l_x	Number dying during age interval $d_{n\,x}$	In the age interval $L_{n\,x}$	In this and all subsequent age intervals T_x	Average number of years of life, remaining at beginning of age interval e°_x
	0–1	0.0237	100,000	2,372	97,868	6,683,185	65.8
	1–5	.0037	97,628	359	389,637	6,585,317	67.5
	5–10	.0025	97,269	244	485,693	6,185,660	63.7
	10–15	.0026	97,025	251	484,575	5,709,967	58.9
	15–20	.0082	96,774	795	482,066	5,225,392	54.0
	20–25	.0112	95,979	1,079	477,232	4,743,326	49.4
	25–30	.0102	94,900	969	472,072	4,266,094	45.0
	30–35	.0114	93,931	1,074	467,079	3,794,022	40.4
	35–40	.0160	92,857	1,498	460,815	3,326,943	35.8
	40–45	.0243	91,369	2,223	451,699	2,966,128	31.4
	45–50	.0372	89,146	3,319	438,068	2,414,429	27.1
	50–55	.0580	85,828	4,974	417,452	1,976,361	23.0
	55–60	.0894	80,854	7,232	387,127	1,558,909	19.3
	60–65	.1336	73,622	9,335	344,544	1,171,782	15.9
	65–70	.1885	63,787	12,023	289,624	827,238	13.0
	70–75	.2718	51,764	14,069	224,037	537,614	10.4
	75–80	.3509	37,695	13,229	155,322	313,577	8.3
	80–85	.4556	24,466	11,148	93,387	158,255	6.5
	85 and over	1.0000	13,320	13,320	64,868	64,868	4.9

Source: U.S. Public Health Service, "Life Tables" in *Vital Statistics of the United States, 1969,* Vol. 2, Sec. 5, p. 7.

To the present, the United States has been singularly lucky in this respect. The total number of deaths of American citizens due to the wars in Korea and Vietnam has been negligible. Even in World War II the number of battle deaths among armed forces personnel was less than 300,000,[1] which was only a small fraction of the almost 6 million deaths occurring normally to civilians during the less-than-four-year period in which the United States was at war.[2] Various other nations have not shared our luck—Russia is a prime example. The French demographer Jean-Noel Biraben has estimated that in the Soviet Union during World War II the crude death rate reached a peak of 53 per thousand in 1942, compared with a rate of 18 per thousand just before the war in 1940.[3] Of course, in certain parts of the Soviet Union the death rate was considerably greater than in the nation as a whole. It has been estimated that in the winter of 1941–42, when Leningrad was besieged by the German Army, approximately one-third of that city's three million inhabitants died of cold and hunger.[4]

A future war might well result in a level of mortality substantially above that previously experienced. In 1963, United States Secretary of Defense Robert McNamara testified that in the event of nuclear war, fatalities in the United States might approach 100 million persons, or somewhat more than half our total population.[5]

Nations usually exhibit important differences in mortality according to social class. For the United States, data on this topic are not plentiful since many of the usual indicators of social class are not available from death certificates. Nevertheless, standard mortality ratios by educational attainment and by family income for the adult population of the United States have been computed by means of matching death certificates for the months of May through August 1960 with the April 1960 Census schedules. Although these ratios may not be of the highest validity (since only 77 percent of the death certificates could be matched to the Census schedules), their pattern is striking. To illustrate, among white males 25

1. U.S. Bureau of the Census, *Statistical Abstract of the United States, 1966* (Washington, D.C.: Government Printing Office, 1966), p. 260.

2. U.S. Public Health Service, *Vital Statistics of the United States, 1964*, Vol. 2, Part A (Washington, D.C.: Government Printing Office, 1966), p. 2.

3. Jean-Noel Biraben, "Essai sur l'evolution demographique de l'U.R.S.S.," *Population*, 18, No. 2a (June, 1958), pp. 41–44.

4. Leon Gouré, *The Siege of Leningrad* (Stanford, Calif.: Stanford University Press, 1962), p. 218.

5. Testimony before the House Armed Services Committee, February, 1963, quoted in speech by Senator George McGovern (D., S.D.), *Congressional Record*, 2 August 1963.

to 64 years of age, those with less than five years of schooling had a standard mortality ratio of 115 whereas those who were college graduates had a ratio of 70; among white females of this age group, the corresponding ratios were 160 and 78.[6]

Data on infant deaths by social-class indicators have also been made available for the United States. A mail questionnaire was sent to a probability sample of parents of legitimate live births in 1964–66 and a second probability sample of parents of infants dying before age one during these same years. From the data collected, death rates by family income, father's education and mother's education were computed. For both whites and blacks of each sex striking differences by social-class indicators were shown. For example, for white female infants, the number of deaths per 1,000 live births was 22.4 when family income was less than $3,000 as compared to 17.4 when family income was $10,000 or more; and 29.2 when mother's education was eight years or less as compared to 16.0 when mother's education was sixteen years or more.[7]

For the United States the differential mortality of whites and nonwhites is of interest. This differential is at least in part a reflection of social class, since a very large proportion of all nonwhites are of lower social class. Currently, nonwhites have a considerably higher mortality rate than whites. The mean expectation of life at birth for white men and women in the United States in 1969 was 71.3 years, whereas that for nonwhite men and women was only 64.3 years. Furthermore in 1969 the death rates for nonwhites from 20 to 49 years of age were approximately double those of whites.[8] Nevertheless, the mortality differential between whites and nonwhites is now less than it used to be. In 1969 the mean expectation of life at birth of nonwhites was only 10 percent less than among whites, whereas in 1900 it had been 31 percent lower.[9]

Mortality differences among nations are still substantial although the range in mortality level among nations is considerably less now than it was before World War II. Although expectation of life in the less developed nations cannot usually be known precisely since so many of them lack a complete registration of deaths, it can be reasonably estimated that the people of several nations in Africa currently have an expecta-

6. Evelyn Kitagawa, "Social and Economic Differentials in Mortality in the United States, 1960" in International Union for the Scientific Study of Population, *International Population Conference*, London, 1969 (Liege, Belgium, 1971), pp. 980–95.

7. Brian MacMahon et al., "Infant Mortality Rates: Socioeconomic Factor," *Vital and Health Statistics*, Series 22, No. 14, p. 12.

8. U.S. Public Health Service, "Life Tables" in *Vital Statistics of the United States, 1969*, Vol. 2, Sec. 5, p. 8.

9. Helen C. Chase, "White-Nonwhite Mortality Differentials in the United States," *Health, Education, and Welfare Indicators* (June 1965) pp. 27–38.

tion of life at birth of only thirty-five years or less. In Burma, the Khmer Republic (Cambodia), India, Indonesia, Pakistan, and Vietnam the expectation of life at birth is estimated to be no more than about fifty years. On the other hand, in the United States, Canada, Australia, New Zealand, Japan, the Soviet Union, and most of the European nations, the mean expectation of life at birth for both sexes is about seventy years or more. The lowest mortality in the world is found in Norway, the Netherlands, and Sweden, where the expectation of life at birth for males (at least seventy-one years) is about four years greater than in the United States, and that for females (around seventy-six years) is about two years greater than in the United States.[10]

In at least some parts of Europe mortality decline has been reliably reported since the latter half of the eighteenth century. This decline, however, was quite gradual until the latter part of the nineteenth century. Within the past century the reduction in mortality in Europe and the other now-developed nations has been an event of truly phenomenal magnitude. To illustrate: in 1900 the average expectation of life at birth in the United States was only 47.3 years, compared to 70.4 years in 1969. In the United States and other nations with reduced mortality, the declines in infancy and childhood, and among young adults, have been much greater than for older persons. For example, the death rate for white infants under one year of age in the United States declined from 159 per thousand in 1900 to 19 per thousand in 1969 or by 88 percent. Similar percentage declines were attained for all ages below thirty-five. On the other hand, the death rate for white persons eighty-five years old and over declined by only 19 percent.[11]

The trend in mortality in the less developed nations cannot be plotted as precisely as in the developed nations. However, it is clear that a major reduction in mortality occurred in many nations in a very short time-period following World War II. For example, in Chile, where death registration is quite complete, the crude death-rate declined from 19.3 per thousand in 1945 to 15.0 in 1950, and was further reduced to 12.3 by 1960. Deaths of infants under one year of age per 1,000 live births declined from around 150 in 1945 to slightly over 100 in 1950 and later years, and even sharper declines were obtained in the mortality of children and young adults.[12] In India the crude death-rate probably declined from about 27 per 1,000 in 1941–50 to about 19 per thousand in

10. *United Nations Demographic Yearbook, 1971* (New York: United Nations, 1972, pp. 746–65.

11. Chase, "White-Nonwhite Mortality Differentials," pp. 27–38; U.S. Public Health Service, "Life Tables", p. 8.

12. *Recent Mortality Trends in Chile*, National Center for Health Statistics, Series 3, No. 2 (Washington, D.C.: U.S. Public Health Service, 1964).

1958–59.[13] But perhaps the most dramatic decline in mortality occurred in Ceylon, where the crude death-rate declined from around 20 per 1,000 in 1940–44 to less than 10 per 1,000 in 1958.[14]

In the more recent past, mortality rates have apparently stabilized in many countries. In the United States the expectation of life at birth has remained essentially constant since 1954.[15] Even in Chile, where mortality is still quite high compared to that in the developed nations, there has been little decline in age-specific mortality rates since 1953.[16] The reasons for this recent stabilization will be discussed in the next section.

DETERMINANTS OF MORTALITY

Mortality is a consequence both of *morbidity* (sickness) and of the *case-fatality* rate—that is, of the proportion of sick persons who die. Whereas *curative medicine* is aimed specifically at reducing case-fatality rates, *preventive medicine* (the most important components of which are adequate nutrition, environmental control, immunization, and health education) may help to reduce either morbidity *or* case-fatality. Let us first discuss the contributions of each of the various types of preventive medicine, and then the role of curative medicine.

Although famine, a common cause of death in former times, has in recent years been largely eliminated by the speedy transport of food to areas temporarily bereft of their own supply, *level of nutrition* is still an important determinant of mortality. Recent studies have provided con-clusive proof that a very important cause of high mortality levels among children under five is an inadequate diet, especially with respect to pro-tein. For example, in a Mayan area of Guatemala, Gordon, Behar, and Scrimshaw (a team of public-health physicians and nutritionists) con-ducted an experiment in which over a four-year period the children of one village were given a daily high-protein dietary supplement consisting of milk, a banana, and *Incaparina* (a product described in chapter 2).[17]

13. *Population Bulletin of the United Nations, No. 6—1962* (New York: United Nations, 1963), pp. 37–38.

14. Ibid., p. 38.

15. U.S. Public Health Service, "Life Tables," p. 12.

16. *Recent Mortality Trends in Chile*, National Center for Health Statistics, Series 3, No. 2 (Washington, D.C.: U.S. Public Health Service, 1964), p. 1.

17. Nevin S. Scrimshaw, "The Effect of the Interaction of Nutrition and Infection on the Pre-School Child" in *Pre-School Child Malnutrition: Primary Deterrent to*

The mortality rates of children under three years of age in this village were then compared to those of children in a nearby control village and to the mortality rates existing in the test village before the experiment. Although little reduction was secured in the death rate of babies less than one month old, among infants one to eleven months old the death rate was only 19 per thousand, compared to 106 per thousand in the control village, and 113 per thousand in the test village prior to the experiment. For children six to eighteen months old the death rate in the experimental village was 30, compared with 97 in the control village, and at nineteen to thirty-six months of age the death rates were 10 and 25 respectively. The improved diet of the test village resulted not only in a lower incidence of such diseases as diarrhea and measles, but also in a lessening of their severity, so that both morbidity *and* case-fatality rates were reduced. If such inexpensive sources of protein as Incaparina can be widely used, clearly they will have a great effect on the mortality of infants and young children in the less developed nations. Achieving widespread acceptance of Incaparina or a similar substance will, however, demand a widespread program of health education.

Various measures of *environmental control* are also of great aid in preventing disease. The quarantine of persons affected by infectious disease, one of the earliest public-health actions ever to be enforced by governmental action, is an example of effective environmental control. Two other major measures of environmental control are adequate disposal of sewage, and a pure water supply. In the opinion of one expert, these two have done more for the health of human beings than any other hygienic measures.[18]

The English barrister Edwin Chadwick was the person most responsible for the idea that proper sanitation should be the responsibility of governments. In *The Sanitary Conditions of the Working Population of Great Britain*, published in 1842, Chadwick persuasively argued the causal connection between sanitary care and disease, and urged that each local unit of government appoint a physician as a salaried health officer. The Public Health Act of 1848, passed largely at Chadwick's urging, provided for the first time a statutory authority for such health officers.[19] An additional impetus for improving water supplies was obtained when John Snow, a London physician, proved that the incidence of cholera

---

Human Progress (Washington, D.C.: National Academy of Sciences—National Research Council, 1966), pp. 63–73.

18. C. Fraser Brockington, *Public Health in the Nineteenth Century* (Edinburgh: E. & S. Livingstone, 1965), p. v.

19. Ibid., pp. 136–63.

during the epidemic of 1848 was especially high in those areas of the city where the drinking water was of lowest quality.[20] A similar discovery with respect to typhoid fever was soon made by another English physician, William Budd.[21]

More recently, a major advance in environmental control has been obtained through the use of insecticides such as DDT to kill the mosquitoes which carry malaria. Mass sprayings of DDT in tropical nations soon after World War II were responsible for large-scale reductions in mortality from this cause within a very short time.

Immunization against specific infectious diseases began with Edward Jenner's discovery in 1771 that smallpox could be prevented by injection of material obtained from persons infected with the milder disease of cowpox. In the latter half of the nineteenth century the bacteriological and viral theory of disease was developed by Louis Pasteur, Robert Koch, and others. Pasteur, who also invented the process we call "pasteurization," dramatically proved (particularly to his less knowledgeable and imaginative critics) that immunization against certain diseases could be accomplished by inoculation with a live but attenuated organism, when he developed first his famous vaccine which saved thousands of European sheep and cattle from the scourge of anthrax, and then the celebrated vaccine which prevents rabies from developing in human beings. Since the late nineteenth century, vaccines have been developed for many if not all of the important infectious diseases.[22] All told, mass immunization has played a major role in making death from infectious disease exceedingly uncommon in the developed nations, and in causing a substantial decline in mortality from such diseases in the less developed nations.

Mortality levels may also be influenced by programs of *health education*. Instruction concerning proper nutrition and personal hygiene has without a doubt played an important role in the mortality decline during the past century. Future declines in mortality from such diseases as lung cancer and heart disease may depend on further education concerning smoking, diet, and exercise.

The technology of curative medicine has also made great advances since the middle of the nineteenth century. One of the most important, made around 1865, was Joseph Lister's development of antisepsis (antiseptic methods), which greatly reduced the possibility of infection during

20. Charles Wilcocks, *Medical Advance, Public Health and Social Evolution* (Oxford: Pergamon Press, 1965), p. 105.

21. Ibid., p. 106.

22. Ibid., pp. 118–34.

and after surgery.[23] Another major advance, begun in 1928, was the development of antibiotics, which was initiated by Alexander Fleming's discovery that the mold *penicillium notatum* could kill staphylococci.[24] Then, too, widespread use of antibiotics during and after World War II led to very substantial reductions in deaths from wounds and from many diseases such as tuberculosis, bubonic plague, typhoid, and typhus.

At present, mortality from infectious disease is quite rare in the developed nations and has been very greatly reduced in the poorer nations. (In the developed countries, most deaths now occur from degenerative disease.) Because little progress has been made in further reducing mortality from these diseases, there has been little change in mortality levels in the developed nations since about 1955. In the less developed nations, perhaps the chief drawback to a reduction in mortality is malnutrition. A second impediment to mortality reduction in the poorer nations is the great scarcity of physicians, auxiliary health personnel, and hospitals and clinics, particularly in the rural areas where most of the populace lives. Better health facilities and more adequate nutrition will both depend on the degree of economic advance which these nations can make, although perhaps, if eating habits can be changed and if products such as Incaparina can find mass acceptance, better nutrition can be obtained at little additional monetary cost.

THE SOCIAL EFFECTS OF SOCIETAL DIFFERENCES IN MORTALITY

It is possible that the dramatic decline in mortality since the end of the nineteenth century has evoked more changes in social structure than any other single development of the period. However, there has been so little research that any discussion must be speculative.

Contemporary citizens of developed nations rarely encounter death, except among the aged. This situation contrasts greatly to that which prevailed in these nations formerly. To illustrate how different the situation was in our own country during the past, let us note some of the bereavements suffered by three presidents of the United States and their families. George Washington's father died when George was only eleven. Upon her marriage to George, Martha Washington was a twenty-six-year-old widow. She had already borne four children, two of whom had died in infancy; and of her two surviving children, one died at age

23. Ibid., pp. 115–17.

24. Ibid., pp. 201–9.

seventeen and the other in early adulthood. Thomas Jefferson lost his father when Tom was only fourteen. His wife Martha had also been previously widowed when she married Jefferson at the age of twenty-three, and died herself only eleven years later. Of the six children that Martha bore to Tom, only two lived to maturity. Abraham Lincoln's mother died when she was thirty-five and he was nine. Prior to her death she had three children; Abraham's brother died in infancy, and his sister in her early twenties. Abraham Lincoln's first love, Anne Rutledge, died at age nineteen. Of the four sons born to Abraham and Mary Todd Lincoln, only one survived to maturity.[25] Clearly, a life with so many bereavements was very different from most of our lives today.

A seemingly direct consequence of the reduction in the frequency of bereavement is a decline in the institutions of mourning. In his book *Death, Grief, and Mourning*, the English anthropologist Geoffrey Gorer points out that at the beginning of the twentieth century there were strict rules of etiquette that the bereaved must observe toward others and that others should show toward him. At present, however, neither the bereaved nor the circle of his acquaintances knows quite how to act toward the other, and in fact a common reaction is to try to deny the very existence of the bereavement. In Gorer's opinion, the lack of bereavement ritual and the frequent attempt to act as if the death had not occurred combine to retard healing and prolong the period of the bereaved's emotional upset.[26]

Another apparent consequence of the decline in mortality is a change in the character of religion. In their book *Popular Religion*, a content analysis of trends in popular inspirational literature in the United States since 1875, Schneider and Dornbusch point out a sharp decline in the emphasis placed on how religion will benefit one in the next world, and a marked increase in the emphasis on how religion will aid one in this world.[27] Evidently, the intensity of popular feeling concerning an afterlife has waned. Probably a very important reason for wanting an afterlife is to reunite oneself with friends and relations who have already died. In a high-mortality society, persons of all ages have many close friends and relatives who have recently died; in a low-mortality society, only the elderly find themselves in this position. Thus mortality decline should reduce the general concern with immortality.

25. *The 1973 World Almanac* (New York: Newspaper Enterprise Association, 1973), pp. 774–77.

26. Geoffrey Gorer, *Death, Grief, and Mourning* (Garden City, N.Y.: Doubleday, 1965).

27. Louis Schneider and Sanford M. Dornbusch, *Popular Religion: Inspirational Books in America* (Chicago, Ill.: University of Chicago Press, 1958).

It is also possible, however, that extremely negative attitudes toward traditional religion may also abate with the reduction of mortality. This seemingly self-contradictory action might be based thus: supposing that the experience of prematurely losing one's parent, spouse, or child would provoke in certain individuals severe doubt that there can be a deity who is both benevolent and omnipotent, the smaller the number of persons who have such an experience, the fewer will be the number who will develop or tend to cling to extremely negative attitudes toward such a belief.

A third possible consequence of mortality decline may be a change in family structure. When there is a large probability of early widowhood and orphanhood, it is hazardous for a nuclear family—i.e., a married couple and its children—to isolate itself too far from its kin group. This is because the death of either the father or the mother would make it very difficult for the orphaned children to receive proper rearing and support. Thus, in high-mortality societies we commonly see the nuclear family strongly dependent on some larger kin-group. By contrast, in the low-mortality, developed nations of today, the nuclear family often lives at a considerable distance from other kin, and its ties with relatives, although present, are considerably weaker than they would be in a society with high mortality. In turn, the possibility of a large number of relatively isolated nuclear families has important implications for the process of economic development. A high economic level is not possible without an elaborate division of labor, and much geographical mobility is necessary if very specialized occupational positions are to be filled by the best possible people. Hence, a high level of mortality, by impeding the possibility of a relatively isolated and independent nuclear family, also hinders the process of economic development.

A fourth possible consequence of high mortality may be a reduced intensity of certain interpersonal ties. In a society wherein many children will die before reaching the age of five, parents may frequently steel themselves for the possibility of their child's early death by forbidding themselves to develop a strong emotional attachment. The same may also apply to marriage. Arranged marriages are common in high-mortality societies, whereas in societies with low mortality, marriage is commonly contracted by free choice to a person for whom one has a strong emotional commitment. In a society in which a strong love relationship might soon be disrupted by death, there should be less dissatisfaction with a system of arranged marriages than in societies where mortality is low. Conversely, one may speculate that the pressure for easy divorce may increase as mortality declines, since the number of years one must expect to live jointly with one's spouse becomes so much longer.

A fifth possible consequence of societal differences in mortality is a difference in orientation to time. It may be hypothesized that when mortality is high, individuals tend to have a weaker orientation toward the future and a stronger orientation toward the present than when mortality is low.[28] If so, this may have further effects on the degree of achievement motivation in the society, since achievement always involves a sacrifice of present values for future goals. Furthermore, where mortality is high, parents may be loath to make sacrifices for the future success of their children, since the probability of the child's living to maturity is by no means certain.

Finally, the level of mortality in a society appears to influence its fertility directly. We shall examine in detail some of the reasons for this effect in the following chapter.

28.   For a similar view see Stephen Enke, *Economics for Development* (Englewood Cliffs, N.J.: Prentice-Hall, 1963), p. 405.

CHAPTER 5
FERTILITY

FERTILITY MEASUREMENT

We noted in the last chapter that because death rates vary considerably by age, an accurate comparison of mortality among different populations demands a control for differences in age composition. The crude birth-rate (again, births per 1,000 of the total population) does not adequately provide this control.

For females, the period of fecundity (i.e., the biological capacity to conceive and bear children) may extend from about age fourteen to almost age fifty. It is impossible to be more precise, since there is considerable individual variation in the reproductive span, factors such as diet may be important in explaining variations in the span among different populations, and—last but hardly least—a full study of the topic has never been made. We do know, however, that the fecundity of women is distinctly higher in the middle years of the reproductive period than at other times, and that adolescents and women past the age of forty have relatively low fecundity.[1] But even less is known about the reproductive span of men than of women. One can state rather imprecisely that the production of spermatozoa begins at puberty and gradually increases until full maturity is reached, and that after the age of forty there is a decline in the amount of active sperm-

1. Moni Nag, *Factors Affecting Human Fertility in Nonindustrial Societies: A Cross-Cultural Study* (New Haven, Conn.: Department of Anthropology, Yale University, 1962), pp. 104–20.

atozoa. Of course, some men never achieve a high rate of sperm production, others experience an early decline in production, and still others possess abundant spermatozoa even in extreme old age.[2]

The implication of these biological facts for fertility measurement is that the proportion of the total female or male population capable of reproduction is often no more than about half. Furthermore, within the group of reproductive age, differences in age composition must be taken into account.

Although it is possible to compute fertility rates for both males and females, presentation of female fertility rates is much more common than that of male rates. This is largely a matter of convention and the availability of data. Both male *and* female fertility rates *should* be computed for those populations which, because of war losses or other reasons, have a very abnormal sex ratio. This is appropriate because whenever there is an excess of females, male fertility rates are apt to be much higher than those for females, whereas when men are in surplus, female rates may exceed those for males. Moreover, one must always be aware that fertility differentials which exist for females may not exist in the same manner for males.

The most exact comparison of fertility in two different populations is obtained by presenting *age-sex specific birth-rates*—i.e., the ratio of the births to individuals of a given age and sex to the total number of same-sexed individuals at that age, for each age-sex group for which reproduction is biologically possible. It is often more convenient, however, to compare two populations according to one summary measure of fertility, and several such summary measures are available. The *general fertility rate* for females is defined as "the number of births per 1,000 women 15 to 44 years of age." This measure provides considerable but not perfect control for differences in age composition. A general fertility rate can also be computed for males; the most commonly used base is men 15 to 54 years old. The *total fertility rate*, which can be computed for either women or men, is simply the summation of age-sex specific birth-rates over each age in which reproduction is possible. For females the formula for the total fertility rate is

$$\sum_{x=15}^{49} b_x$$

where b_x is the number of children borne per woman of age x. A variant of the total fertility rate is the *gross reproduction rate*, which can also be

2. A. S. Parkes, ed., *Marshall's Physiology of Reproduction*, Vol. 1, Part 2 (Boston, Mass.: Little, Brown, 1966), p. 81; and Moni Nag, *Factors Affecting Human Fertility*, p. 105.

computed either for women or for men. For females the gross reproduction rate is

$$\sum_{x=15}^{49} b^f_x$$

where b^f_x is the number of female children borne per woman of age x.

The gross reproduction rate for males is, similarly, the summation, over each age in the male reproductive period, of the ratio of births of male children fathered by men of a given age to the total number of men of that age. The gross reproduction rate for each sex is therefore approximately half the value of the total fertility rate for that sex. The total fertility rate and the gross reproduction rate both offer an exact control for differences in age composition, since in the computation of either of these measures each age-group is always given the same "weight" as any other age-group.

In discussing mortality we mentioned that two types of measures were possible: period measures and cohort measures. The same distinctions can be made for fertility measures. For example, the *period total fertility rate* for females in 1970 would consist of a summation of age-specific birth-rates for women of each age in 1970, whereas the total fertility rate for the birth cohort of 1919–20 would consist of a summation of the birth rate for 10-year-old girls in 1930, 11-year-olds in 1931, and so on, up to and including 49-year-old women in 1969. It is an empirical observation that the fluctuation over time in period fertility measures is considerably greater than the fluctuation in measures for birth cohorts. This is because period fertility rates are greatly affected by changes in the timing of births. A decline in the mean age at childbearing temporarily inflates the period total fertility rates (or their variants, the *period gross reproduction rates*) even though there is no change in the total fertility or gross reproduction of any birth cohort. On the other hand, a rise in the average age of childbearing temporarily deflates the period rates even though there is no change for any birth cohort. It is now widely recognized that the decline in the age at childbearing in the United States in the 1950s produced period fertility rates that were somewhat higher than the rates which can be expected for any birth cohort.

Even when the registration of births is imperfect, as in many of the less developed nations, and the direct measurement of fertility lacks validity, much useful fertility data can be obtained from census data. The proportion of the total population under age 15 is a very good general indicator of the level of fertility in a population; equally suitable is the ratio of children under five to women 15 to 49 years of age. In many censuses, women are questioned concerning the number of children they have ever borne. The number of children ever born to women 45 to 49 years of age as determined from the census bears a very close relation to the total fertility rate for the birth cohort born 45 to 49 years before the census.

We have covered in some detail the simpler and more frequently used measures of fertility. Before moving to another topic, it would be appropriate to point out that there are other fertility measures in quite common use. These include fertility rates for married and unmarried persons, for married persons by duration of marriage, and rates by parity (i.e., the number of live births a woman has already had) and by duration of parity (the number of years since a woman has had her last child).

DIFFERENTIAL FERTILITY

There is a very extensive body of data describing differences in fertility among nations at a given time; within a single nation over time among geographic areas within a single nation, such as its rural and urban areas; and among such social categories as individuals with varying amounts of educational attainment, or income, or of different occupation, religion, or ethnic group. However, much of the existing data are difficult to interpret because it is not certain that the difference in question is caused by a difference in the classifying variable or in some variable associated with it. For example, the fertility of Jews in the United States is lower than that of any other major religious group, but controversy has developed as to whether the cause of this lower fertility is associated with the Jewish culture itself or whether it is merely a result of the fact that Jews differ substantially from other Americans in their residence, occupation, or some other factor.[3]

Although the interpretation of fertility differences must be done with caution, a knowledge of some of the actual variations in fertility among different populations and strata is valuable, if only to give an idea of the possible range in human fertility which may be observed. Currently, the Hutterites—the aforementioned communalistic religious group now residing in South Dakota, North Dakota, Montana, and the prairie provinces of Canada—apparently hold the world's record for high fertility. An analysis of the fertility of a Hutterite community conducted by Eaton and Mayer showed that, among married women 45 to 54 years of age, the mean number of children ever born was 10.6. This high number was

---

3.   See Ronald Freedman et al., "Socio-Economic Factors in Religious Differentials in Fertility," *American Sociological Review* (1961), 26:4, 608–14; and Calvin Goldscheider, "Fertility of the Jews," *Population Index* (1966), 32:3, 330.

achieved despite the fact that these women first married at an average age of more than twenty years. If allowance were made for the reproductive time lost by marriage delay, one would estimate that the average woman of this group has the biological capacity to bear at least twelve children. The period gross reproduction rate of all Hutterite women (married and unmarried) in 1946–50 was 4.00.[4] Although a few populations, such as those of the eighteenth-century British[5] and French colonies[6] of North America have approximated the Hutterite figure, fertility in most nations, including the less developed nations, currently falls considerably short of the record set by the Hutterites. The other end of the fertility range is exemplified by Sweden, wherein the female gross reproduction rate in 1970 was 0.94.[7] For females in the United States in 1972 the gross reproduction rate was almost as low, about 0.99.[8]

Let us now look at some of the commonly described types of fertility differentials. We shall successively discuss fertility differences (1) between the developed and less developed nations at the current time, (2) in the now developed nations over time, (3) between urban and rural areas, (4) according to social class, and (5) according to religious or ethnic group.

In general, the nations with the lowest per-capita income have the highest fertility, and vice-versa. For example, India has a female gross reproduction rate of about 2.70, whereas in the developed nations the female gross reproduction rate usually ranges from about 1 to 2.9[9] However, the relationship between national levels of income and of fertility is not invariant. Certain nations with a relatively high income, such as Venezuela, have very high fertility, and other nations with a relatively low income, such as Greece and Japan, have very low fertility. Moreover, the relation between national fertility level and per-capita income is not so pronounced as the relation between fertility and infant mortality, or

4. Joseph Eaton and Albert J. Mayer, "The Social Biology of Very High Fertility among the Hutterites: The Demography of a Unique Population," *Human Biology* (1953), 25:3, 206–64.

5. Wilson H. Grabill et al., *The Fertility of American Women* (New York: John Wiley, 1958), pp. 5–13.

6. Jacques Henripin, *La Population Canadienne au debut du XVIII Siecle* (Paris: Institut National D'Etudes Demographiques, 1954).

7. *Population Index* (April-June 1972), 38:2, 235–44.

8. Estimated from data contained in U.S. Bureau of the Census, *Current Population Reports*, Series P-25, No. 499 (May 1973), p. 2.

9. *United Nations Demographic Yearbook, 1965* (New York: United Nations, 1966), pp. 605–17; *United Nations Demographic Yearbook, 1969* (New York: United Nations, 1970), pp. 474–77.

even between fertility and per-capita newspaper circulation (an accurate and widely available index of average educational level). Furthermore, when the relation of income to fertility is considered in a simultaneous statistical analysis holding constant the effects of four other variables, per-capita income is found to have a positive rather than a negative relation with the national fertility level.[10]

In all of the economically developed nations the level of fertility is now substantially less than what it was a hundred or more years ago. However, the decline in fertility has not been an altogether regular process. The fertility decline for the white population of the United States from 1800 to 1972, shown in figure 2, illustrates this irregularity very well. Fertility decline was quite regular from 1800 to 1935; thereafter we observe the pronounced "baby boom" of the 1940s and 1950s, followed by the very sharp drop in fertility in the 1960s and early 1970s. Analysis of the long-term trend in fertility in several of the developed nations has demonstrated that variation in the business cycle has a marked effect on fertility. Other things being equal, fertility tends to rise above the long-term trend when times are exceptionally prosperous, especially for the young adults just entering into parenthood, and to fall when the economy is depressed.[11]

In most nations fertility, particularly when measured for females, is substantially higher in rural areas than in urban. For example, in the United States in 1970 the average number of children ever born to all women 35 to 44 years old was 2.8 in urbanized areas (cities of 50,000 population or more and their suburbs), and 3.5 among farm residents.[12] Part of this difference resulted because a smaller proportion of women had ever married in urbanized areas than on farms. However, the difference between urbanized areas and farms in the United States was almost as pronounced among married women as among all women, and among married women the difference was present regardless of the size of the husband's income.[13] Substantial urban-rural fertility differences,

10. David M. Heer, "Economic Development and Fertility," *Demography* (1966), 3:2, 423–44.

11. Virginia Galbraith and Dorothy S. Thomas, "Birth Rates and the Interwar Business Cycles," *Journal of the American Statistical Association* (December, 1941), 36, 465–76; Dudley Kirk, "The Relation of Employment Levels to Births in Germany," *Milbank Memorial Fund Quarterly* (April, 1942), 40:2, 126–38; and Richard Easterlin, *The American Baby Boom in Historical Perspective* (New York: National Bureau of Economic Research, 1962).

12. U.S. Bureau of the Census, *1970 Census of Population*, Final Report PC(1)-D1, pp. 675–76.

13. Ibid., pp. 181–86.

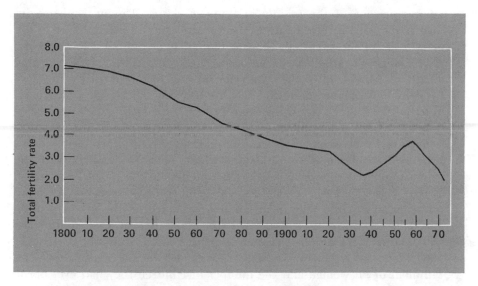

Figure 2 Total Fertility Rate for the White Population of the United States, 1800–1972. Sources: Ansley J. Coale and Melvin Zelnik, *New Estimates of Fertility and Population in the United States* (Princeton, N.J.: Princeton University Press, 1963), p. 36; U.S. Public Health Service, *Vital Statistics of the United States*, Vol. I, Section 1, p. 7; and estimates by the author derived from U.S. National Center for Health Statistics, *Monthly Vital Statistics Reports*, 19, No. 12 (1971) and 21, No. 12 (1973).

at least for females, are also found in all of the European nations and in Latin America.[14] In parts of Africa and Asia, however, there appears to be much less urban-rural difference in fertility.[15] The reason for this has not been fully clarified. The lack of a strong urban-rural fertility difference here may be due in part to the fact that, unlike the situation in Western nations, the cities attract many single men rather than single women. Another factor may be a higher level of infant and childhood mortality in the cities, which tends to increase the number of children born, if not the number of children surviving.

Many studies have noted that fertility in the developed nations tends to be highest among persons of the lower social classes, and lowest

14. *Population Bulletin of the United Nations, No. 7—1963* (New York: United Nations, 1965), pp. 122–34.

15. Ibid., and Warren C. Robinson, "Urbanization and Fertility: The Non-Western Experience," *Milbank Memorial Fund Quarterly* (1963), 41:3, 291–308.

among persons of the middle and upper classes. Recent evidence in-
dicates that this inverse relationship was much more pronounced in the
early years of the twentieth century than it is at present. However, the
data available to study social-class differences in fertility are not entirely
adequate. Almost all of the data refer only to female fertility, and very
little is known about social-class fertility differences for males. Moreover,
much of the female data is for those currently married, which may differ
somewhat from data applicable to the total female population. Fertility
data by social class are further confounded by several other factors (most
notably by differences in residence) which must be controlled if the
intrinsic relation between social class and fertility is to be ascertained.
In the United States the poorest and least educated persons are more
often found in rural than in urban areas, and within the urban population a larger proportion of the working class than of the middle class
has a farm background. Although for the United States as a whole in
1960 there was a generally inverse relation between the educational attainment of all women and the number of children they had ever borne
by ages 35 to 44, this relationship was less pronounced in the urbanized
areas than in the nation as a whole.[16] Furthermore, in the United States
in 1962, among married women 35 to 44 years old residing in urban areas
and with no farm background, the difference in fertility according to
level of educational attainment, although slight, was somewhat U-shaped
rather than inverse.[17]

   In the years following World War II the previously existing inverse
relationship between husband's income and fertility began to change
toward a direct relationship. This change can best be illustrated for
white married women living in urbanized areas. In 1960 among such
women fifty years old and over, those with husband's income of $10,000
or more had fewer children ever born than the women in any other income class. In contrast, among the women 30 to 39 years old in 1960,
those with husband's income of $10,000 or more had a higher number
of children ever born than the women with husbands in any other income
class.[18] On the other hand, following 1960 there was a reversal in this
trend toward a direct relationship between husband's income and fertility. For the United States as a whole among all married women 35 to 44
years of age, women whose husband's 1969 income was $15,000 or more
had an average of 3.0 children whereas women whose husband's 1969

16. U.S. Bureau of the Census, *1970 Census of Population*, pp. 100–101.

17. Otis Dudley Duncan, "Farm Background and Differential Fertility," *Demography*
(1965), 2, 240–49.

18. U.S. Bureau of the Census, *United States Census of Population*, 1960, Vol. 2,
Part 3A, p. 182.

income was less than $2,000 had an average of 3.3 children ever born. Among that subset of these women living in urbanized areas, there was almost no relation between husband's income and fertility; the average number of children ever born was 3.0 for those women with husband's 1969 income of $2,000 or less and also 3.0 for those with husband's 1969 income of $15,000 or more. The relationship in 1970 between children ever born and husband's 1969 income for white women varied somewhat by state. In most of the highly urbanized states in the Northeast, there was essentially no relationship between husband's 1969 income and the number of children ever born. Conversely in other states, particularly in the South and Southwest, there was a substantial inverse relationship.[19]

Many studies show that within a nation there are often substantial fertility differences among its different religious or ethnic groups. In many cases we do not have enough data to test whether the difference is caused by some feature of the group's culture, or whether it is merely an accidental result of the group's residence, level of mortality, literacy, income, or some other accidental factor. However, a detailed study of the Protestant-Catholic fertility differential in the United States in 1955 indicated that this difference was accentuated when Protestants and Catholics are equated on such factors as urban-rural residence, income, and educational attainment.[20] On the other hand, many almost wholly Catholic nations in Europe have quite low fertility. In explanation of this aparent contradiction, Lincoln Day has hypothesized that Catholic fertility is elevated only in nations where Catholics feel they are subject to political persecution by non-Catholic groups.[21] In such nations, the laity follow more closely the doctrine of the Church with regard to birth control; moreover, the Catholic clergy are also more likely to promote the large-family ideal.

A good example of the effect of other confounding factors on the fertility of an ethnic group is obtained by examining the relative fertility of American blacks. For the United States as a whole in 1960 the average number of children ever born to women 35 to 44 years old was 2.4 for whites and 2.8 for blacks. In New York State, on the other hand, the respective figures were 2.1 and 1.8.[22]

19. U.S. Bureau of the Census, *Census of Population: 1970*, Final Report PC(2)-3A, pp. 246–247 and Final Reports PC(1)-D2 through PC(1)-D52, Table 162.

20. Freedman et al., "Socio-Economic Factors in Religious Differentials in Fertility."

21. Lincoln H. Day, "Natality and Ethnocentrism: Some Relationships Suggested by an Analysis of Catholic-Protestant Differentials," *Population Studies* (March 1968), 22, 27–50.

22. U.S. Bureau of the Census, *United States Census of Population, 1960*, Vol. 2, Part 3A, pp. 1, 20–21, and 296.

MECHANISMS DIRECTLY
AFFECTING FERTILITY

A causal analysis of fertility differentials may involve a great number of factors and complicated chain reactions. It is therefore appropriate to make a systematic classification of the mechanisms which directly affect fertility and through which all other factors must operate. An excellent categorization of these mechanisms has been devised by Kingsley Davis and Judith Blake.[23] Their most basic concept is that the birth of a child is not possible unless: (1) sexual intercourse has occurred, (2) intercourse has resulted in pregnancy, and (3) pregnancy has been brought to successful term. Building on this concept, they have devised a list of eleven variables which directly affect fertility. They term these "intermediate variables" since any other variables which may affect fertility must ultimately act through one of these. We shall list these now under their own section heading and then, since societies differ very greatly in their values on at least some of these variables, we shall consider all eleven in some detail.

Intermediate Variables
Affecting Fertility

I.   Factors affecting exposure to intercourse
   A.   Those governing the formation and dissolution of unions in the reproductive period
      1.   Age of entry into sexual unions
      2.   Permanent celibacy; proportion of women never entering sexual unions
      3.   Amount of reproductive period spent after or between unions
         a.   When unions are broken by divorce, separation, or desertion
         b.   When unions are broken by death of husband
   B.   Those governing the exposure to intercourse within unions
      4.   Voluntary abstinence
      5.   Involuntary abstinence (from impotence, illness, and unavoidable but temporary separations)
      6.   Coital frequency (excluding periods of abstinence)
II.   Factors affecting exposure to conception
      7.   Fecundity or infecundity, as affected by involuntary causes

23.   Kingsley Davis and Judith Blake, "Social Structure and Fertility: An Analytic Framework," *Economic Development and Cultural Change* (1956), 4, 211–35.

8. Use or non-use of contraception
   a. By mechanical and chemical means
   b. By other means
9. Fecundity or infecundity, as affected by voluntary causes (sterilization, subincision, medical treatment, etc.)

III. Factors affecting gestation and successful parturition
   10. Foetal mortality from involuntary causes
   11. Foetal mortality from voluntary causes

1. *Age of entry into sexual unions.* In the nations of European culture a couple is not supposed to marry until the husband is able to support a wife and family. In preindustrial Europe the age of marriage was relatively low, but beginning at least as early as the eighteenth century the age at marriage began to rise. This rise was so substantial that actual fertility levels were reduced far below their biological potential. During the twentieth century, age at marriage in Europe has been declining concomitant with the increased acceptance of birth control within marriage.[24] Ohlin has suggested that the earlier rise in the European age at marriage could plausibly be explained by the decline in mortality, since the average man now had to wait longer before inheriting land or advancing from his apprenticeship.[25]

In many Asian nations, on the other hand, the age at first marriage has always been very early, since marriages are arranged and the husband is not expected to support his family entirely by his own efforts.

In recent years Ireland has presented the extreme in late age at marriage. In 1961, 45 percent of all females 25 to 29 years old had never married, and 67 percent of males. The other extreme is India, where in the same year and in the same age-group the proportion of women who had never married was only 2 percent and the proportion of males a mere 17 percent.[26]

2. *Permanent celibacy.* A rather high proportion of permanent celibates is frequent in nations which have a late average age at marriage. Ireland again represents the extreme of high proportions celibate. In Ireland in 1961, in the 45- to 49-year age-group, 22 percent of all women and 31 percent of all men had never married.[27]

3. *Amount of reproductive period spent after or between unions.* To some extent in all societies, actual fertility is reduced below the biologically

24. J. Hajnal, "European Marriage Patterns in Perspective," in David V. Glass and D. E. C. Eversley, eds., *Population in History* (Chicago, Ill.: Aldine Publishing Co., 1965), pp. 101–43; and Ansley J. Coale, "Factors Associated with the Development of Low Fertility: An Historic Summary," Paper #WPC/WP/194, delivered at the United Nations World Population Conference, Belgrade, Yugoslavia, 1965.

25. G. Ohlin, "Mortality, Marriage, and Growth in Pre-industrial Populations," *Population Studies* (March, 1961),14:3, 190–97.

26. Data for both Ireland and India are from *United Nations Demographic Yearbook, 1963* (New York: United Nations, 1964), pp. 726–27 and 730–31.

27. Ibid., pp. 730–31.

maximum level because part of the reproductive period is spent after or between sexual unions. Where monogamy is institutionalized, it is almost inevitable that a certain proportion of widows never remarry, since there are almost always considerably more widows than widowers, and many widowers prefer to remarry never-married women. Periods of separation between marital unions are also important in some societies in reducing fertility. Perhaps the best-known locus of this practice is Jamaica.[28] There, few sexual unions are undergirded with legal marriages, and many of the consensual unions break up. The breakup may be caused by marital (legal or otherwise) incompatibility, or in many cases may occur simply because the woman does not want to incur the chance of an additional pregnancy.

4. *Voluntary abstinence.* Certain primitive societies enjoin periods of voluntary abstinence on special ceremonial occasions. Almost all societies enjoin a period of abstinence during late pregnancy and also during the early postpartum period. The former has no detrimental effect on fertility and the latter has little since almost all women have very low biological fecundity during this time. Of the various forms of voluntary abstinence, the "rhythm method" probably has the greatest effect on fertility. This method of birth control demands abstinence in the days before and around the time of ovulation, which generally occurs around the midpoint of the menstrual cycle. When properly practiced, it will reduce conception rates by a rather large amount.

5. *Involuntary abstinence.* In a few societies a large proportion of men must absent themselves from their wives periodically to obtain gainful labor. For example, this is often the case in highland Peru, where many of the men migrate to the coast during the season when sugar cane is harvested.[29]

6. *Frequency of intercourse.* Much theoretical evidence suggests that this variable may be rather important in determining differences in fertility between individuals. Whether or not it affects the fertility of different populations is another matter. It is possible, however, that factors such as diet, temperature, humidity, and the prevalence of certain enervating diseases may have effects on the average frequency of sexual intercourse in different populations. This is clearly a field where we need much more information than we now have.

7. *Fecundity or infecundity as affected by involuntary causes.* Several factors may affect the probability of conception, given the fact that intercourse occurs at a specified frequency. On a worldwide basis, perhaps the chief of these is the incidence of venereal disease, particularly gonorrhea. Venereal disease affects the fecundity of both men and women. Empirical studies have shown that it is a very frequent cause of childlessness in parts of tropical Africa, and in the recent past it has also apparently been a very important cause of childlessness among American blacks.[30] A survey

28. See Judith Blake, *Family Structure in Jamaica: The Social Context of Reproduction* (New York: The Free Press, 1961).

29. David M. Heer, "Fertility Differences between Indian and Spanish-speaking Parts of Andean Countries," *Population Studies* (July, 1964), 18:1, 71–84.

30. Reynolds Farley, "Recent Changes in Negro Fertility," *Demography* (1966), 3:1, 188, 203.

of the Belgian Congo (now Zaire) conducted in the latter part of the 1950s showed that in certain areas up to 35 percent of all women 45 years old and over had never borne a child, and that the incidence of childlessness was very strongly correlated with the incidence of venereal disease in the area.[31]

A second factor which may involuntarily affect fertility is altitude. It is quite likely that high altitude, for example, depresses to some extent the fecundity of the inhabitants of the Indian-speaking areas of Bolivia, Peru, and Ecuador.[32]

Finally, extreme hunger has been found to cause amenorrhea (and hence temporary sterility) in women, and a reduced sperm-count in men.[33]

Modern medical science has made considerable progress in reducing the proportion of persons who are involuntarily childless. The use of antibiotics to cure venereal disease has been very important in this respect. Another advance has been the use of artificial insemination to impregnate women whose husbands are sterile. New drugs have recently been developed which stimulate ovulation and allow certain women to conceive who otherwise would probably never be able to do so.

8. *Use or non-use of contraception*. According to popular belief, contraception is the most important of all of the intermediate variables affecting fertility. Actually, although there is no doubt that contraception is very influential in reducing levels of fertility, it is definitely not so overwhelming a contribution that the other variables can be ignored.

Contraceptive techniques date back to antiquity.[34] The simplest technique, coitus interruptus (i.e., withdrawal of the penis from the vagina just before ejaculation) is mentioned in the Old Testament. At least among those who choose to use it, coitus interruptus is highly effective, and it is still a very important means of contraception in Europe. A condom made of linen was invented in the sixteenth century; the first manufacture of rubber condoms took place in the late nineteenth century; and appeared in the 1930s. The condom is now one of the most popular and effective forms of contraception in the world. The diaphragm, invented in the 1800s, has also become a popular and highly effective method of contraception.

In the early years of the 1960s a revolution in contraceptive technology occurred with the widespread acceptance of two new methods— the oral contraceptive and the IUD (intrauterine device)—whose use could be separated from the act of intercourse. The oral contraceptive is coitus-independent and is also the first contraceptive that is almost completely effective when used according to instructions. By 1965 it had

31. A. Romaniuk, "Fecondite et sterilite des femmes Congolaises," in *International Population Conference, New York, 1961* (London: International Union for the Scientific Study of Population, 1963), 2, 109–17.

32. W. James, "The Effect of Altitude on Fertility in Andean Countries," *Population Studies* (July, 1966), 20:1, 97–101.

33. Ancel Keys et al., *The Biology of Human Starvation* I (Minneapolis: University of Minnesota Press, 1950), 749–63.

34. For a very complete account of the history of contraceptive practices, see Norman Himes, *Medical History of Contraception* (New York: Gamut Press, 1963).

become the most widely used contraceptive in the United States: in that year, among married white women eighteen to thirty-nine years old, 24 percent had used the pill as their most recent method of contraception.[35] The intrauterine device has the great advantage that once it is inserted, the wearer has no need to make any further contraceptive efforts. It is not perfectly reliable, but is probably at least as effective as the condom or diaphragm when these are used during each act of intercourse. The IUD has been the principal contraceptive employed in the family planning programs of many of the Asian nations.

9. *Fecundity or infecundity as affected by voluntary causes.* The surgical operations of tubal ligation in the female and vasectomy in the male provide an individual permanent freedom from further parenthood without destroying sexual pleasure or creating any alternations in personality. Of the two operations, vasectomy is the simplest and least costly. At one time vasectomy was much less popular than tubal ligation, but its prevalence increased dramatically during the decade of the 1960s so that by 1970 the number of sterilized husbands was actually greater than the number of wives who had experienced a tubal ligation. By 1970, among couples where the wife was 35 to 39 years of age, the proportion of couples in which either husband or wife had had a sterilizing operation for contraceptive purposes was 18 percent, as compared with only 11 percent in 1965.[36] Currently, medical researchers are attempting to perfect a method of vasectomy which will allow an effective reversing operation. Under present methods the chance of reversing the effect of a vasectomy is only around 50 percent. If a surely reversible method of vasectomy can be obtained, it may become one of the most widely used methods of birth control among couples who have completed their desired family size.

On a worldwide basis, prolonged breast-feeding is one of the most important means by which a woman may temporarily reduce her fecundity. Women are sterile during their period of postpartum amenorrhea and a short period of anovulatory cycles following the resumption of their menses. Prolonged lactation has a pronounced effect on the length of the period of postpartum sterility. Potter estimates that the period of postpartum sterility averages thirteen months in a population which engages in prolonged lactation, and only four months in a population with no lactation.[37]

10. *Fetal mortality from involuntary causes.* On the average, about 20 percent of all known pregnancies are spontaneously aborted.[38] There is much individual variation in the proportion of pregnancies which mis-

35. Charles F. Westoff and Norman Ryder, "United States: Methods of Fertility Control, 1955, 1960 and 1965," in *Studies in Family Planning*, No. 17 (February, 1967).

36. Larry L. Bumpass and Harriet B. Presser, "Contraceptive Sterilization in the U.S.: 1965 and 1970," *Demography* (November 1972), 9:4, 531–48.

37. Robert G. Potter, Jr., "Birth Intervals: Structure and Change," *Population Studies* (November, 1963), 17:2, 155–66; and Robert G. Potter et al., "A Case Study of Birth Interval Dynamics," *Population Studies* (July, 1965), 19:1, 81–96.

38. Potter, "Birth Intervals: Structure and Change."

carry, but little is known how populations may vary in this respect. 11. *Fetal mortality from voluntary causes.* Induced abortion is one of the most important means of birth control. Primitive and hazardous methods of abortion have been practiced throughout human history. Modern surgical methods make induced abortion a very safe operation when conducted properly.[39] However, in those nations where abortion is still illegal, the operation is frequently hazardous to health, and even to life.

Abortion can now be performed with a very minimum amount of legal restriction in the United States, Japan, Denmark, the United Kingdom, the USSR, the People's Republic of China, Poland, Czechoslovakia, the German Democratic Republic, Hungary, and Yugoslavia. In many of these nations the frequency of induced abortion is very high. In Hungary, for example, the number of abortions officially reported is considerably higher than the number of live births.[40] The recently-invented suction-pump method of abortion, which reduces by half the proportion of cases with postoperative complications, has now been widely adopted in the United States, mainland China, and the East European nations, replacing the method of dilatation and curettage.[41]

It is very difficult to obtain exact statistics on the incidence of abortion in nations where it is illegal except for stringent medical indications. For the United States during the 1950s when abortion was still almost entirely illegal, a group of leading experts estimated that the number of illegal abortions was between 200,000 and 1,200,000 per year.[42] A study recently conducted in Chile concluded that approximately one in every three or four pregnancies in that nation was interrupted by abortion.[43] And authoritative claims have been made that the number of illegal abortions in France and Italy approximates the number of live births, but the evidence on which these claims are based is quite fragmentary.

39. Christopher Tietze, "The International Medical Experience," in *Abortion Experience in the United States*, ed. H. J. Osofsky and J. D. Osofsky (New York: Harper and Row, 1973); "Mortality, Morbidity in Legal Abortions Drop as Women Learn Early Procedures Safer," *Family Planning Digest*, 2, No. 3 (May 1973), pp. 8–9.

40. A. Klinger, "Abortion Programs," in *Family Planning and Population Programs*, ed. Bernard Berelson et al. (Chicago, Ill.: University of Chicago Press, 1966), pp. 465–76.

41. Christopher Tietze, "Two Years' Experience with a Liberal Abortion Law: Its Impact on Fertility Trends in New York City," *Family Planning Perspectives* (Winter 1973) 5:1, pp. 36–41; Anibal Faundes and Tapani Luukainen, "Health and Family Planning Services in the Chinese People's Republic," *Studies in Family Planning* (July 1972), 3:7 Supplement, pp. 165–76; K. H. Mehlan, "The Socialist Countries of Europe," in *Family Planning and Population Programs*, ed. Bernard Berelson et al. (Chicago, Ill.: University of Chicago Press, 1966), pp. 208–9.

42. Mary G. Calderone, ed., *Abortion in America* (New York: Hoeber-Harper, 1958), pp. 178–80.

43. Mariano Requena, "Social and Economic Correlates of Induced Abortion in Santiago, Chile," *Demography* (1965), 2, 33–49.

FACTORS AFFECTING THE DECISION
TO HAVE CHILDREN

The eleven intermediate variables we have cited are concerned with the means by which change in the fertility of a population can be affected. An understanding of these variables gives one a good idea of the *involuntary* biological factors which constrain fertility. However, the level of fertility itself can be explained only when we also consider *voluntary* decisions concerning childbearing. Biological factors place a natural upper limit on the fertility of the individual, but the individual can reduce his own fertility to whatever degree he chooses. Even in primitive societies excess fertility can always be avoided, though the price for doing so may be very great. To consider two extreme examples: (1) couples may decide to refrain from sexual intercourse to avoid a further pregnancy; and (2) the pregnant woman can always decide to abort the fetus even at the risk of her life.

An excellent conceptual scheme for the analysis of the factors affecting the decision to have children has been devised by the economist Joseph Spengler.[44] He considers the decision to have an additional child a function of three variables: (1) the preference system, (2) the price system, and (3) income. Provided we define these terms in a broader sense than they usually receive in the economic literature, these three concepts provide for a complete classification of all factors that affect this decision. The *preference system* simply describes the value a married couple places on an additional child relative to the value of all other goals they might achieve without having that child. The *price system* delineates the cost of an additional child relative to the cost of attaining all other goals that might be achieved if the decision were made not to have another child. Costs must be very broadly defined and must include not only monetary costs but expenditures of time and effort as well. *Income* must also be broadly defined to include not only monetary income but the total amount of time and energy that a couple has for pursuit of all of its possible goals in life. (Because the term *resources* fits the definition more closely than the term *income*, I shall henceforth use the term *resources*.) Given these definitions of the three variables affecting the decision to have an additional child, we can presume that the probability of deciding in favor of another child will vary directly with the relative value anticipated from that child, inversely with the predicted relative cost, and directly with the amount of resources foreseen as available for all goals.

44. Joseph J. Spengler, "Values and Fertility Analysis," *Demography* (1966), 3:1, 109–30.

Spengler's scheme is very useful in analyzing the long-term changes in fertility which have occurred over the last century in the now-developed nations, the fertility differences which now exist between the developed and less-developed nations, and fertility differentials within a nation.[45] Although all of these might be discussed, I shall like to concentrate attention on how this scheme helps to clarify the long-term trends in fertility within the now-developed nations.

The now developed nations have a long history of increasing per-capita monetary income. They also have a long history of decreasing hours devoted to gainful employment and increasing amounts of leisure time. If there had been no change in either price or preference system, one might then have expected that the long-term trend in fertility would have been upward. Clearly, since over the long run fertility has tended downward, changes in the preference and price system must have discouraged rather than encouraged fertility to an extent that counterbalanced the elevating effects of increased money and leisure time. On the other hand, for a long period during the 1940s and 1950s in all of the developed nations which did not suffer severely from World War II (the United States, Canada, Australia, and New Zealand), we observe a substantial fertility rise. At least for the United States it has been well documented that this period of rising fertility was also one of very rapid rise in monetary income for young adults.[46] It is therefore plausible to presume that during this period the elevating effect of rising income more than counterbalanced any depressing effects of changes in the preference or price system.

In the last hundred years or so, there have undoubtedly been several changes in the preference system in the now-developed nations which have tended to reduce desired family size. One of the most important changes is probably the decline in mortality. As emphasized earlier, the secular (long-term) decline in mortality has had greater relative effect in infancy and childhood than among adults. Therefore, if fertility had not declined, the reduction in mortality would have tended to increase somewhat the number of living children per living parent. This may be illustrated by presenting ratios of children to adults of parental age for typical stable populations differing only in mortality.[47]

45. Of course a complete explanation of fertility differentials must also take into account changes in such nonvolitional biological factors as the incidence of venereal disease, and nutritional status.

46. Richard Easterlin, *The American Baby Boom in Historical Perspective* (New York: National Bureau of Economic Research, 1962).

47. A stable population is one with a calculable and unchanging rate of growth and a calculable and unchanging age composition. Stable populations are more fully described in chapter 7.

For example, the United Nations estimates that for a stable population with a gross reproduction rate of 2.5 and a life expectation at birth of 20 years, the ratio of population under 15 years to that 15 to 59 years is 0.56; whereas when the expectation of life at birth is increased to 70 years with no change in the gross reproduction rate, this ratio is increased to 0.83.[48] Thus, as the level of mortality declined, one would expect the value of an additional birth to wane.

A second possible effect of mortality reduction on the preference system relates to a possible connection between the level of mortality and the amount of emotional energy that parents invest in each of their children. It may be supposed that the pain of bereavement at a child's death is directly proportional to the amount of emotional energy that the parents have invested in that child. Therefore, where mortality levels are high, one might expect parents, in the interests of self-protection, to place relatively little emotional involvement in any one child. Since parents have limited amounts of emotional energy, a reduction in mortality, by encouraging parents to place more libido in the existing children, should reduce their desire to have an additional child.[49]

A third reason why mortality reduction should lead to a lower preference for additional children is obtained if one assumes that parents want to be reasonably certain of having a specified minimum number of children survive to maturity. Where mortality is high, one cannot be sure that any of one's existing children will survive to maturity. When mortality is as low as it is in the now-developed nations, parents can be highly certain that their child will survive from birth to maturity. Thus, a decline in mortality reduces the value of an additional child as insurance for the possibility that one or more of the existing children may die. The effect of mortality reduction in this respect can even be quantitatively measured. If one assumes (1) that each couple is capable of bearing twelve children, (2) that a perfect means of birth control is available and utilized, and (3) that all couples want to be 95 percent certain of having at least one son who will survive to the father's sixty-fifth birthday, the gross reproduction rate (a computer simulation study shows) will fall from 5.2 when the expectation of life at birth is 20 years, to 0.95 when the expectation of life rises to 74 years.[50]

---

48. United Nations, Department of Economic and Social Affairs, *The Aging of Populations and its Economic and Social Implications* (New York: United Nations, 1956), pp. 26–27.

49. This idea was first advanced in an oral communication by Dr. Laila Sh. El Hamamsy, Director of the Social Research Center, American University in Cairo, Egypt.

50. David M. Heer and Dean O. Smith, "Mortality Level, Desired Family Size, and Population Increase," *Demography* (1968), 5:1, pp. 104–21.

A second long-term change in the preference system relates to the value which parents can achieve from the productive labor of their children. In the agrarian society of the United States in the eighteenth century, with the supply of land practically unlimited, children could be a very productive asset to their parents at a very early age. When the amount of land per capita declined, as it did in the United States during the nineteenth century, the value to the farmer of the labor of an additional child probably declined correspondingly. Moreover, in all of the now-developed nations, industrialization resulted in a further substantial reduction in the value of child labor. Although such labor was quite common in many of the early factories, the situation of the child in the factory was much less satisfactory than if he were working under the direction of his father on the family farm. As a result, much moral sentiment developed against child labor, and in all of the developed nations legislation emerged restricting it. The productive value of child labor was still further reduced by compulsory education laws which, becoming increasingly severe, lowered still further the productive value of an additional child to its parents.

A third long-term change in the preference system relates to the change in the institutions which provide support for the elderly. In the preindustrial period and in the early stages of the Industrial Revolution, the elderly could expect to receive financial support only from their own kin—mainly from their own sons. Gradually, business corporations and governments developed social-security schemes for the aged and for widows. With the full development of these schemes, it was no longer necessary for parents to bear enough children so that they would have one or more sons to support them in their old age. Thus the value to parents of bearing additional children was further diminished.

A fourth change in the preference system was a decline in the rewards which could be expected from society at large for bearing a large number of children. When mortality was high, a high rate of fertility was a positive necessity if the population was not to decline. Governmental and religious authorities who did not wish to see the nation's population decline encouraged a high level of fertility. As mortality declined, the necessity for a high level of fertility merely to maintain the existing level of population subsided. As a result, many governments and religions have changed their attitudes from one favoring large families to one opposing them.

A fifth possible change in the preference system may have resulted because economic development tends to promote a shift from allocation of social status by ascription to allocation by achievement. Where status is ascribed at birth, one need spend little effort in advertising one's status; whereas when status is achieved, its level tends to be transitory, and individuals may develop an intense need for conspicuous consumption (i.e., a compulsion to show off possessions that are not necessarily needed or wanted, but are regarded as status symbols) to demonstrate their rank. If the preference for conspicuous consumption increases, then the preference for children, who do little to publicize one's status, must decline.[51]

Over the past century the development of new and improved methods of birth control has not only reduced the relative preference for children but has also increased their price relative to that of other goals. When available methods of birth control are crude and undeveloped, or when knowledge of better methods is lacking, the decision not to have an additional child involves a high expenditure of resources as well as substantial inconvenience, interference with sexual pleasure, and even the hazard to life and health incurred by resort to a primitive means of abortion. During the 1960s, for example, the increasing use of the highly effective oral contraceptive in the United States and other nations may have been one of the major reasons for their sharp fertility decline.

Economic development has produced other changes in the price system affecting desired family size. One of the most important concomitants of economic development has been urbanization. By raising population densities, urbanization usually causes an increase in the relative price of living space. Since rearing children demands considerable amounts of living space, the relative cost of children rises with each increase in its relative price. Although we may presume that over the past hundred years or so the relative cost of living space has in general been increasing, it is possible that the rise has not been invariant. One may speculate that in the United States in the 1940s and 1950s, increasingly widespread use of the automobile, together with governmental policies which subsidized home ownership, made possible the acquisition of suburban homes at a relative cost probably substantially lower than that during previous decades. Part of the American Baby Boom of the 1940s and 1950s may be explained by this short-term change in the relative cost of living space. Conversely, during the late 1960s and early 1970s the very high interest rate for home mortgages increased the effective cost of living space for young married couples and may have been an important factor in the sharp decline in fertility during those years.

Another factor affecting desired family size is that the labor cost of child care tends to rise in relation to the labor cost of producing material goods. While economic development makes possible a much

51. For an argument of this type with respect to the middle class of England during the late Victorian period see J. A. Banks, *Prosperity and Parenthood* (London: Routledge & Kegan Paul, 1954).

larger production of factory goods per man-hour of labor, the number of man- and woman-hours necessary to supervise and socialize a child has certainly not declined, and in fact most probably has risen. Therefore, when a married couple is deciding whether or not to have another child, they can assume that an additional child will burden the wife with the responsibilities of child care for about three more years, or more precisely by the number of years intervening between this birth and the last one. Moreover, with another child to supervise, she will have to work harder during the period when the older children are still under her care. This increased effort must be set against the possible remuneration from a job. Since the amount of material goods which can be bought with each hour of labor outside the home has steadily increased with each advance in national economic level, there has been a substantial secular increase in the price of child-care services relative to the price of material goods.

A final long-term change in the price system which affects the decision to have children concerns the quality of education which parents demand for their children and which is socially imposed. A society increasingly oriented to a complex technology requires that children be given an increasingly lengthy education, and parents recognize more and more that their own child will be at a substantial disadvantage unless his education meets society's new norm. Even where the direct cost of education is met by the state, longer education increases the cost to the parent in terms of more years of child dependency. Hence the secular increase in the standard of education has also helped to depress family size.

DIFFERENTIAL REPRODUCTION
AND THE LEVEL OF INTELLIGENCE

Population genetics studies the "gene pool'" of a population and the factors that cause it to change. One of the most important problems in human population genetics is to measure the changes, if any, which may be taking place in the *genetic* component of human intelligence. The term "genetic" is emphasized because it has already been clearly demonstrated that intelligence-test scores are influenced not only by the character of one's genes but also by one's environment.

The eugenics (eugenic = well-born) movement has been concerned not only with investigating changes in the human gene pool, especially as they might affect intelligence, but also with advocating programs which would encourage the reproduction of presumably genetically superior elements of the population and discourage the reproduction of the supposedly inferior. One of the principal founders of the eugenics movement was the English scientist Francis Galton, who published his first ideas advocating a eugenic program in 1865. In the late nineteenth and early twentieth centuries many eugenicists became convinced that the average level of innate human intelligence was declining, at least within the developed nations. They further predicted that this decline, if unchecked, would have disastrous consequences for society.[52]

In support of their belief that the mean level of innate intelligence was declining, the eugenicists argued that intelligence was at least in part genetically determined (i.e., determined by the character of one's genes at conception). Furthermore, they believed that genetic intelligence was inheritable—that is, that the genetic intelligence of the child would tend to vary directly with that of his parent. On these two points the eugenicists were in concurrence with the views of most scientists. In addition, the eugenicists believed that the growth rate of the more intelligent segment of the population was lower than that of the less intelligent portion. This belief was principally derived from the following three pieces of indirect "evidence."

First of all, numerous studies in all developed nations showed an inverse relation between the socio-economic status of the husband and the fertility of his wife. Secondly, numerous studies demonstrated an inverse relation between a woman's educational attainment and the number of children she had borne. The third source of evidence came from studies relating the intelligence of children, as measured by psychological tests, to the number of their siblings. These studies all showed an inverse relation between intelligence and sibling number.[53]

To make inferences from any of these data to the growth rates of population segments differing in intelligence obviously demands many additional assumptions. For example, from the first set of data one must assume that unmarried people can be ignored and that socio-economic status and intelligence are so highly correlated that they can be regarded as identical; to make inferences from the second set one must assume that education and intelligence are extremely closely associated, and furthermore that the population growth-rates for women in each intelligence grouping are the same as those for men. To make inferences from the third set of data, one has to assume that the intelligence of parents is very closely associated with that of their children, that couples who have

52. For the history of the eugenics movement see C. P. Blacker, *Eugenics: Galton and After* (London: Gerald Duckworth, 1952), and Mark H. Haller, *Eugenics: Hereditarian Attitudes in American Thought* (New Brunswick, N.J.: Rutgers University Press, 1963).

53. For a review of these studies see Anne Anastasi, "Intelligence and Family Size," *Psychological Bulletin* (May, 1956), 53:2, 187–209.

no children can be ignored, and that there are no environmental factors operating among children in large families to reduce their measured intelligence.

Although the evidence for declining intelligence was only inferential, many noted demographers, psychologists, and geneticists made quantitative estimates of how rapidly the level of intelligence was declining. For example, in 1934 Lorimer and Osborn estimated that the average IQ in the United States was declining one point per generation.[54] Other writers estimated that the drop per generation was as much as four points.[55]

Opportunities soon arose to determine whether or not intelligence-test scores were actually declining. Much to the surprise of many experts, all of the large studies designed to investigate generational trends in intelligence found that the intelligence level was increasing. The largest of these studies was conducted in Scotland, where the entire group of eleven-year-old children was first tested in 1932 and then again in 1947. The average IQ in the later test was found to average about two points higher than in the earlier one.[56]

A rise in measured intelligence is not necessarily contradictory with a decline in the genetic component of intelligence. It is plausible that an increase in favorable environmental factors, such as a high level of education among parents, and hence more intellectuality in the home, had counterbalanced the adverse factor of declining genetic inheritance. Moreover, there was no doubt that the level of education among parents was continually rising, and if this increased education among parents did indeed increase the measured intelligence of their children, it could cause the IQ of the later generation to be considerably higher than that of the earlier.

Clearly, the question of declining innate intelligence could not be settled without further data. The next step was to measure the intelligence of a group of children and then find out how many offspring they had had by the end of their reproductive years. For example, if one begins with a group, or cohort, all tested at age ten, one should first subdivide it according to intelligence-test score. For each subgroup of like scores, one should then find out the average number of children borne or fathered who survived to age ten. One would then have the growth

54. Frank Lorimer and Frederick Osborn, *Dynamics of Population* (New York: Macmillan, 1934), chapter 8.

55. Anastasi, "Intelligence and Family Size," p. 97.

56. Scottish Mental Survey Committee, *The Trend of Scottish Intelligence* (London: University of London Press, 1949).

rate of each intelligence grouping over the span of a generation. However, this would not yet tell us whether or not the annual growth-rate of subgroups of differing intelligence varied, since the length of generation may vary by level of intelligence. We may define the *mean length of generation* as "the average age of parents at the birth of their children." If more intelligent people receive more education and marry later than the less intelligent, their average generation length will be longer. Therefore, in order to obtain the annual growth-rate for each intelligence grouping, one must divide the generational growth-rate by the mean length of generation.

In 1963, Bajema completed the first study, which closely conformed to the previously mentioned ideal "research design."[57] Bajema began with a group of 1,144 native white individuals born in 1916 and 1917 who had been tested for intelligence in the sixth grade of the Kalamazoo public school system. He was able to obtain life-history data for 979 of these 1,144, and was able to determine for each individual the number of his or her children who survived to age one.

One of the most original aspects of Bajema's study is his investigation of subsequent mortality dependent upon sixth-grade IQ. Bajema found that the higher the IQ, the higher the proportion who survived to age 45. For example, among individuals with an IQ of 120 or higher, 96 percent survived, whereas among those with an IQ of less than 80, only 87 percent survived. Among survivors to age 45, Bajema found that the group with an IQ of 120 or more had the highest number of children (2.62), whereas the group of lowest intelligence (IQ less than 80) had the smallest, only 1.65. An important reason why the lowest-IQ group had so few children on the average was that substantial proportions had never married and/or had never had children.

Although the survivors to age 45 with an IQ of 120 or more had the highest average number of offspring, they were closely followed by the survivors with an IQ of 80 to 94. Thus, survivors of highest intelligence, and those of less-than-average intelligence, each had higher fertility than survivors of near-average intelligence, while those with distinctly subnormal intelligence had the lowest fertility of all. For all persons, including those who did not survive, there was a slight tendency for IQ to be positively associated with number of offspring.

Bajema also found the average length of generation to be slightly longer in the high-IQ group than in the other groups. Computing the annual growth-rate of each IQ grouping by dividing its average number

57. Carl Jay Bajema, "Estimation of the Direction and Intensity of Natural Selection in Relation to Human Intelligence by means of the Intrinsic Rate of Natural Increase," *Eugenics Quarterly* (December, 1963), 10:4, 175–87.

of offspring by its mean generation length, he found that the group with an IQ of 120 or more had the highest annual growth-rate. The group with an IQ of 80 to 94 had the second highest growth-rate, and the group with an IQ of less than 80 had a negative growth-rate which was distinctly lower than that of the other groups. Incidentally, Bajema found, in common with other studies, a negative correlation between the individual's IQ and the number of his siblings, and also a slight negative correlation between the fertility of his females and their subsequent educational attainment.

Two other studies, with a somewhat less adequate research design, have findings congruent with those of Bajema. One was a large study of siblings and parents of persons committed to the Minnesota State School and Hospital for the mentally retarded;[58] the second was a relatively small study conducted in Cambridge, England.[59] Both studies showed clearly that feeble-minded persons who marry tend to have large families, but that since a high proportion of them never marry, the average number of offspring of the total group of feeble-minded is not large. Both studies also confirmed the relatively high reproduction of the top IQ groups.

The question of whether or not the IQ of the population is declining is still not settled. All of the better studies to date are confined to rather small localized areas and to the experience of birth cohorts who have recently completed their reproductive span. It is possible, for instance, that the average level of intelligence in many nations declined for a considerable period of time but is no longer declining. It is possible again that if we limit attention, as studies so far have done, to persons born in urban areas, there will be a positive relation between IQ and subsequent offspring, but that if attention is expanded to rural areas as well, a negative relation might result. Obviously, many more studies are necessary before we have a clear idea of the differential reproduction of groups varying in measured intelligence. Furthermore, no one has as yet succeeded in isolating the genetic component of intelligence from the important environmental influences which affect IQ tests. Until this feat has been accomplished, we must be cautious both in coming to, and in making deductions from conclusions.

Moreover, we need further research not only on *trends* in innate intelligence but also on the *consequences* of changes thereof. Is a declin-

58. J. V. Higgins et al., "Intelligence and Family Size: A Paradox Resolved," *Eugenics Quarterly* (June, 1962), 9:2, 84–90.

59. John Gibson and Michael Young, "Social Mobility and Fertility," in *Biological Aspects of Social Problems*, J. E. Meade and A. S. Parkes, eds. (Edinburgh: Oliver & Boyd, 1965), pp. 69–80.

ing average intelligence really so harmful, as the eugenicists have blithely assumed? One might perhaps argue that in a future world in which all menial work is performed by computer-controlled machines, only the small minority of persons retained as managers and professionals would need a high level of intelligence. The rest of the population, whose sole role would be that of consumer, might do very well with but a modicum of intelligence.

Furthermore, we should pay attention not only to changes in the *mean value* of intelligence but also to the *distribution* of intelligence. At present most persons are of average intelligence; relatively few are of extremely high or extremely low mental competence. It is possible, however, that we are evolving a population wherein relatively few persons will be of average intelligence—most will be either distinctly bright or distinctly subnormal. This could occur if individuals marry others of similar intelligence, and if persons of average intelligence reproduce at a level below that of the rest of the population, as found in Bajema's sample. Would such a development be good or bad? Given the present state of knowledge, we cannot even attempt an answer.

SIBLING NUMBER
AND CHILD DEVELOPMENT

The advocates of planned parenthood have vigorously proclaimed the advantages of small families for the development of the child. Pro-natalists have asserted just as loudly that children develop best in the atmosphere of a large family. The relation between sibling number and subsequent personality is a question of great importance, but unfortunately to date we know relatively little about it.

In the preceding section we noted that there was a small but negative correlation between the measured intelligence of children and the number of their siblings. Although this negative correlation may be entirely caused by the lower intelligence of the parents of very large families, other interpretations are possible. An alternative explanation is that a large number of siblings reduces contact with adults and hence impedes the development of linguistic abilities and leads to a lowering of measured intelligence. Support for the view that lack of adult contact lowers measured intelligence is provided by data which demonstrate that the average IQ of twins is about five points lower than that of singletons, even within groups homogeneous for family size and socio-economic level.[60] As yet, however, there has been no study which has gathered data

60. Anastasi, "Intelligence and Family Size."

on the IQ of both parents and children together with data on the number of children in the family. Without such a study it is impossible to determine the degree of influence which sibling number exerts on the development of intellectual ability.

A few existing studies are concerned with the effect of number of siblings on the child's personality and on his adjustment to his parents. One of the best of these studies concludes that within each social class the fewer the number of their siblings, the better was the adjustment of adolescents to their parents. Among the "only child" children, 38 percent had a superior adjustment to parents, but among those with five or more siblings only 16 percent had it.[61] According to two other studies, a large number of siblings seemed to have a slightly adverse effect on the child's general social adjustment.[62] One of these studies showed that the negative effect of a large sibling number was greater among working-class children than among middle-class children.[63] This may be related to social-class differences in the frequency of unwanted conceptions.

Unwanted conception must definitely be taken into account in considering the impact of sibling number on child development.[64] In the United States, as recently as 1960 to 1965, 17 percent of all births were unwanted by either spouse at time of conception. Births of higher order were more likely to be unwanted than births of lower order, and unwanted conceptions were more common the lower the socio-economic status of the parents.[65] Although in the succeeding five years, the rate of unwanted births in the United States declined by some 36 percent,[66] unwanted births in the United States still constitute a sizeable fraction of the total. It is quite possible that a large number of siblings has *no* effect on a child's development if *all* of the children have been wanted.

61. Ivan Nye, "Adolescent-Parent Adjustment: Age, Sex, Sibling Number, Broken Homes, and Employed Mothers as Variables," *Marriage and Family Living* (November, 1952), 14:4, 327–32.

62. Glenn R. Hawkes et al., "Size of Family and Adjustment of Children," *Marriage and Family Living*, 20:1, 65–68; and Murray J. Strauss and Diane J. Libby, "Sibling Group Size and Adolescent Personality," *Population Review* (July, 1965), 9:1 and 2, 55–64.

63. Strauss and Libby, "Sibling Group Size and Adolescent Personality."

64. Edward Pohlman, "Results of Unwanted Conceptions: Some Hypotheses up for Adoption," *Eugenics Quarterly* (March, 1965), 12:1, 11–17.

65. Larry Bumpass and Charles F. Westoff, "The 'Perfect Contraceptive' Population," *Science*, (September 18, 1970), 169, pp. 1177–82.

66. Charles F. Westoff, "Changes in Contraceptive Practices among Married Couples," in Charles F. Westoff, ed., *Toward the End of Growth: Population in America* (Englewood Cliffs, N.J.: Prentice-Hall, 1973), pp. 19–31.

On the other hand, even when parents desire a large family, the burden of caring for many offspring may compel them to give less individual attention to each, and hence serve to impede development. Again, further research is necessary.

We may also ask what effect sibling number has on one's opportunity for adult success. A study by Blau and Duncan provides a very good answer.[67] Basing their findings on a probability sample of 20,000 American men between 20 and 64 years of age, they found that the number of siblings was negatively related both to educational attainment and to current occupational level. Although their data revealed sibling number to have less effect on future success than father's education or occupation, they were also able to show that the number of siblings had an effect on adult achievement even after holding constant the effect of father's occupation. Specifically, after controlling for the effect of father's occupation, they demonstrated that men who had been only children had the best chance for high educational attainment and occupational success, that men with one to three siblings had better than average prospects, but that men with four or more siblings were clearly disadvantaged. Their data revealed that almost the sole reason for the greater occupational success of those with fewer siblings was their higher educational attainment. No doubt a major reason for the higher educational level of those men with fewer siblings is simply economic. Parents of small families can better afford to educate their sons than parents of large families. However, if a large number of siblings does exert an adverse influence on IQ or on social adjustment, then these factors may also contribute to the negative relation between sibling number and educational attainment.

67.   Peter M. Blau and Otis Dudley Duncan, *The American Occupational Structure* (New York: John Wiley, 1967), pp. 295–313.

CHAPTER 6
MIGRATION

CONCEPTS AND MEASUREMENT

Measuring migration is somewhat more complicated than gauging fertility or mortality. To measure shifts in usual place of residence from one area to another, several considerations must be taken into account. First of all, the "usual place of residence" must be defined. Although this is no problem for most individuals, an explicit definition must be provided persons with more than one "usual residence," such as college students, members of the armed forces, and inmates of institutions.

Secondly, a careful definition of "place of origin" and "place of destination" is necessary. Because these places can be anything from a particular housing unit to a nation or even a continent, the number of migrants will depend on the terms of the definition. In the United States, for example, the number of persons who change households is much greater every year than the number who move to a new county; and that number, in turn, is larger than the number who move to a different state. The U.S. Bureau of the Census makes a distinction between migrants and movers: *migrants* are persons who move to a new *county*; movers are those who move to a new *household*, whether or not they cross a county line. Another common distinction is made between persons who move between nations, *international migrants,* and those who move within a nation, *internal migrants.*

A third consideration is whether to measure the total number of moves during a given time-period or merely the change in place of residence, if any, from the beginning to the end of the period. Most migration analysts are content with the latter measurement, even though with its use the number of residence changes in a relatively long period, such as five years, will be smaller than the sum of the number of changes of residence recorded each year during that period.

Although a student of migration might be happy with a simple description of the number of persons within an area who have moved into a different subarea (e.g., the number of persons in the United States moving into a new state), he would probably want to know where these migrants were going and whence they had come. For the fifty States and the District of Columbia (making fifty-one units) there are a total of 2,550 possible migration "streams," each characterized by a different state of origin and of destination. This is because for any given state there are fifty different streams of out-migrants and fifty streams of in-migrants. The *gross interchange* between place *A* and place *B* is the sum of the number of in-migrants from *B* to *A* and the number of out-migrants from *A* to *B*. The *net migration* for place *A* from place *B* is the difference between the number of in-migrants from *B* to *A* and the number of out-migrants from *A* to *B*. The *effectiveness of migration* between *A* and *B* is the absolute value of the ratio of the net migration to the gross interchange. Theoretically, this ratio can vary from a value of 1, when all migration is unidirectional, to a value of 0, when the migration streams in each direction are of equal magnitude. Commonly, this ratio is nearer to 0 than to 1.

To measure the *crude rate of migration* to different subareas within a given total area, the number of migrants during the year is divided by the midyear population of the total area. The *rate of out-migration* from a given place of origin during a given year is commonly computed by dividing the number of out-migrants from that place by the midyear population of the place of origin, and the *rate of in-migration* to a given place of destination is computed by dividing the number of in-migrants by the midyear population of the place of destination. The *net migration rate* is perhaps the most commonly computed migration rate. For any given place it is simply the ratio of the net number of migrants to or from the place, divided by its population at midyear. Migration rates standardized for age and sex may also be computed. If the requisite data are available, age-specific migration rates for different years may be combined to produce migration rates for cohorts.

Ideally, migration data should be secured by a registration of all geographical movements. International migration can usually be measured in this way. Several nations, of which Sweden is one, have a compulsory registration of all internal movements. However, to measure internal mobility in the United States, we must make use of census and survey data which ask persons where they lived at some earlier date. Mobility data gathered from this source slightly underestimate the total amount of movement because they ignore persons who move and then die before the time of the survey. For nations with low mortality, such as the United States, this cannot cause any serious bias in the data except for the oldest age-groups.

TRENDS, DIFFERENTIALS, AND MAJOR STREAMS

It is much easier to discuss general trends in mortality and fertility than in migration. One reason is that for migration the relevant data are often not available. A second reason is that trends in migration vary from nation to nation, and there has been no generalized change such as has occurred in mortality and fertility. At any rate, for the sake of brevity we shall confine our discussion to trends in the United States.

For this country, annual data on internal migration are available only since the "year" 1947–48, and since then there has been little variation in the rate of geographical mobility. Approximately 19 percent of the total population has moved every year, about 6 percent have changed their county of residence, and about 3 percent have moved to a new state.[1] Fragmentary data suggest that rates of internal migration prior to 1947–48 were essentially of the same magnitude as they have been since that date.[2]

Statistics on immigration into the United States from abroad are available since 1820. The absolute number of persons moving into the nation reached a peak in 1907, when about 1,300,000 immigrant aliens entered the country. However, there have been several major peaks in the rate of immigration into the United States. The apex of the first peak occurred in 1854, when 428,000 immigrants entered the United States; in that year the rate of immigration was 16.1 per thousand of U.S. population. The apex of the last peak, in 1907, coincided with the acme of the absolute number of immigrants; in that year the immigration rate was 14.8 per thousand. The first of the peak periods corresponds to the "old migration" predominantly composed of Irish leaving their native land because of the potato famine, and Germans, often leaving as po-

1. U.S. Bureau of the Census, *Current Population Reports*, Series P-20, No. 235 (April 1972).

2. Everett S. Lee, "Internal Migration and Population Redistribution in the United States" in *Population: The Vital Revolution*, ed. Ronald Freedman (New York: Doubleday, 1964), p. 127.

litical refugees; the second corresponds to the "new migration," predominantly composed of persons from Italy and Eastern Europe.[3] Heavily restrictive legislation passed in 1921 and 1924 greatly reduced the flow of immigrants to the United States, and decline was further accentuated by the Depression of the 1930s. During that decade the average annual number of immigrants was only about 70,000. After World War II the number of immigrants increased somewhat.[4] In 1971 the number of immigrants was 370,000 and the rate of immigration was 1.8 per thousand.[5]

Age is the major differential in migration rates. The highest rates of mobility and migration are for young adults, but there is a secondary peak among very young children. The reason for two peaks is that frequently the migrating unit is a young married couple with small children. In the United States in 1971 about 41 percent of all persons 20 to 24 years old had changed their residence during the past year, and about 16 percent were migrants to a different county. Among children 1 to 4 years old, 28 percent had changed their residence and 10 percent had migrated across a county line. The lowest proportions of movers and migrants were found among the elderly. Among persons 65 years old and over, only 9 percent were movers and only 3 percent migrants. There was little overall difference in the mobility or migration rates by sex.[6] On the other hand, until recent years males have been predominant among immigrants to the United States.[7]

Within the United States, social-class differences in migration are rather small and somewhat contradictory. Persons with a college education are slightly more prone to migration than others, but males with very low income are somewhat more apt to migrate than men with higher income. Self-employment is an important determinant of migration status. In 1971 only 3 percent of self-employed males migrated across a county line during the preceding year, as compared with 7 percent of wage and salary workers.[8] Evidently, persons with their own business or profes-

3. U.S. Bureau of the Census, *Historical Statistics of the United States: Colonial Times to 1957* (Washington, D.C.: Government Printing Office, 1960), pp. 56–59.

4. Ernest Rubin, "The Demography of Immigration to the United States," *The Annals of the American Academy of Political and Social Science* (September, 1966), 367, 15–22.

5. U.S. Bureau of the Census, *Statistical Abstract of the United States, 1972* (Washington, D.C.: Government Printing Office, 1972), p. 91.

6. U.S. Bureau of the Census, *Current Population Reports*, Series P-20, No. 235 (April 1972).

7. Rubin, "The Demography of Immigration in the United States."

8. U.S. Bureau of the Census, *Current Population Reports*, Series P-20, No. 235 (April 1972).

sional practice are at a distinct disadvantage in a new community, since they have to build up a new clientele. On the other hand, many salaried corporation employees are given reassignments and must migrate on pain of losing their job.

Certain major streams of migration deserve to be mentioned either because they have had important historical consequences or because they otherwise exemplify unusual patterns. One of the earliest streams of migration with historical significance was the westward movement of nomadic tribes in Europe and Central Asia coincident with the fall of the Roman Empire. The many tribes that moved westward during this period included those speaking Celtic, Germanic, and Ural-Altaic languages. As the easternmost tribes moved westward, they pushed forward the tribes in front of them. One possible explanation for this extensive migration is that the grasslands of Central Asia dried up. A second theory is that an expanding Chinese empire disrupted the life of the nomadic tribes near its borders and thus provoked the movement of all the other tribes.[9]

The European and African migration to North America, South America, and Oceania has probably had more important historical consequences than any other migratory stream. This flow began slowly after Columbus's voyage to America. It has been estimated that over 60 million Europeans left for overseas points. However, *net* migration was lower, since many of those leaving Europe later returned.[10] The migration from Africa to the New World was almost wholly a forced migration of slaves. The first slaves were brought to the colony of Virginia in 1619, and in the United States the slave trade was not abolished until 1808. During the period of slave trade, about 400,000 Africans were brought to this country.[11] The impact of this migration is revealed by noting that in 1790, 20 percent of the 4 million persons in the United States were blacks.[12]

As we have seen, the migratory stream from Europe to the United States reached its numerical peak in the first decade of the twentieth century. During this time the rate of immigration from Europe into the United States was 9.2 per thousand, and the emigration rate from

9. B. Bury, *The Invasion of Europe by the Barbarians* (London: Macmillan, 1928); Ellsworth Huntington, *Civilization and Climate* (New Haven, Conn.: Yale University Press, 1924); Frederick J. Teggart, *Rome and China: A Study of Correlations in Historical Events* (Berkeley, Calif.: University of California Press, 1939).

10. United Nations Department of Social Affairs *The Determinants and Consequences of Population Trends* (New York: United Nations, 1953), pp. 98–102.

11. U.S. Bureau of the Census, *A Century of Population Growth in the United States: 1790–1900*, by W. S. Rossiter (Washington, D.C.: Government Printing Office, 1909), p. 36.

12. Conrad Taeuber and Irene B. Taeuber, *The Changing Population of the United States* (New York: Wiley, 1958), p. 71.

Europe to the United States about 2 per thousand.[13] Thus in general the transatlantic migration had considerably more effect on the population of the United States than on that of Europe. However, the emigration rate from Europe to the United States varied considerably from nation to nation and from time to time. During the decade of the Irish potato famine (from 1845 to 1854) the emigration from Ireland to the United States was extremely heavy: about 1.4 million Irish emigrated to the United States from a population which had been in 1841 only a little more than 8 million.[14]

In chapter 3 we discussed the extensive process of urbanization that occurred in the wake of the Industrial Revolution in the developed nations. Migration from rural areas was in large part the cause of this urbanization. Whereas in many nations this migration was almost entirely internal, in the United States before World War I much of the urbanization was accomplished by the passage of peasants from Europe. But in a survey conducted in the United States in 1952 it was revealed that twice as many farm-reared adults were then living off the farm as on the farm, and that one of every three adults not living on a farm had been reared on a farm.[15]

In the United States one of the most significant of the migration streams has been, and continues to be from east to west. In many western states only a minority of the resident population has been born in the state. For example, in California in 1970 only about 47 percent of the resident population was born there.[16] However, one must not think of the interchange between east and west as one of high effectiveness. It is a paradox that a higher proportion of persons born west of the Mississippi River have migrated east of that river than have been born east of the river and migrated westward. Specifically, according to the 1970 census, 7.8 percent of all persons born west of the Mississippi were living east of the river, and only 7.2 percent of those born east of the river were living to the west. The paradox is explained when we look at the absolute number of migrants and consider the absolute numbers born on each side of the river. In 1970, 8.9 million persons born east of the Mississippi were living west of the river, and 4.6 million born west were

13. Calculated from data in *Historical Statistics of the United States*, p. 56, and *The Determinants and Consequences of Population Trends*, pp. 11–13.

14. R. Dudley Edwards and T. Desmond Williams, eds., *The Great Famine* (New York: New York University Press, 1957), pp. 4, 388.

15. Ronald and Deborah Freedman, "Farm-Reared Elements in the Nonfarm Population," *Rural Sociology* (1956), 21, 50–61.

16. U.S. Bureau of the Census, *Census of Population*, 1970, Final Report, PC(2)-2A, pp. 25, 30.

living east, so that the net movement to the west side of the river was 4.3 million, and the effectiveness of the interchange was .32.[17] Nevertheless, since the total population born east of the river was so much greater than that born west of it, the proportion born west and moving east was somewhat higher than the proportion born east and moving west.

Another very significant stream of net migration within the United States has been the northward and westward movement of blacks. This shift began in large scale only during World War I. At that time, northern industrial firms began to recruit labor for jobs which would have normally been filled by newly arrived European immigrants. The movement of blacks out of the South is still continuing. According to the 1970 census, about 24 percent of the total black population born in the South was living in another region, and among those 30 to 34 years of age, about 37 percent were residing outside the region. Of the total black population of the Northeast, 34 percent were born elsewhere—almost entirely in the South; among blacks 30 to 34 years of age in the Northeast, fully 51 percent had been born outside the region.[18]

The migration from Puerto Rico to the mainland United States, of major magnitude since the end of World War II, is of interest because it exemplifies an extremely high rate of out-migration. According to the 1970 census, the combined total of the population of Puerto Rico and of persons in the United States of Puerto Rican birth or parentage was about 4.1 million, of which around 1.4 million were in the United States. Thus 33.9 percent of all Puerto Ricans were on the mainland.[19]

The migration into Israel following World War II is noteworthy because it exemplifies an extremely high rate of in migration. In 1948, when independence was established, the total population of Israel was 650,000. By 1961, after the influx of more than 1 million immigrants, it had risen to 2.2 million.[20]

Perhaps the world's largest gross interchange in a short time-span took place in India and Pakistan following the 1947 partition of British India and the establishment of these two areas as independent states. This movement is also of interest because it was coerced rather than free. In the face of violence, Hindus and Sikhs in Pakistan were compelled to move to India, and Moslems in India to Pakistan. From 1947 through

17. Ibid., pp. 25–26.

18. Ibid., p. 14.

19. U.S. Bureau of the Census, *U.S. Census of Population: 1970*, Final Report PC(1)-A1, p. 48 and Final Report PC(2)-1E, p. 1.

20. Anthony T. Bouscaren, *International Migrations since 1945* (New York: Praeger, 1963), pp. 89–90; and *United Nations Demographic Yearbook, 1965* (New York: United Nations, 1966), p. 113.

1950, 10 million persons migrated from Pakistan to India, and 7.5 million from India to Pakistan.[21]

DETERMINANTS

In the previous chapter we analyzed the determinants of the desired number of children in terms of a preference system, a price system, and the total amount of resources available for all goals. A similar conceptual scheme can be used to analyze migration. Such a scheme can be used not only when social norms concerning migration are permissive, but also when norms and laws either prescribe or proscribe migration. But in the last two cases we must recognize that there may be very heavy penalties for refusal to migrate or unwillingness to stay.

The preference system describes the relative attractiveness of various places as goals for the potential migrant, compared to other goals which his resources would allow him to pursue. An area's attractiveness is the balance between the positive and negative values which it offers.

Let us first consider some of the positive values which may influence a person or family to migrate. Quite understandably, for many migrants the prospect of a better job is one of the most important. In an analysis of internal migration in the United States, Kuznets and Thomas have shown that the net flow of migration within the United States has been (as one might expect) *away from* those states where average income is low, and *toward* those where it is high.[22] Moreover, studies of international migration have shown that the volume of migration *to* a nation naturally tends to be highest when it is near the peak of a business cycle, and *from* it in times of business depression or famine.[23]

Another positive value which may be achieved by migration is a more favorable climate. Florida, for example, has always had a high rate of in-migration despite the fact that its average income has *not* been high. The sunny skies of California exert a similar pull.[24]

Marriage and the continuation of marital ties also are important

21.   O. H. K. Spate, *India and Pakistan: A General and Regional Geography* (New York: Dutton, 1957), p. 119.

22.   Simon Kuznets and Dorothy S. Thomas, "Internal Migration and Economic Growth," in *Selected Studies of Migration Since World War II* (New York: Milbank Memorial Fund, 1958), pp. 196–211.

23.   Brinley Thomas, "International Migration," in *The Study of Population*, Philip M. Hauser and Otis Dudley Duncan, eds. (Chicago: University of Chicago Press, 1959), pp. 526–28.

24.   Kuznets and Thomas, "Internal Migration and Economic Growth."

inducements to migration. In certain of the world's societies, rules of exogamy absolutely compel potential brides and bridegrooms to marry someone from outside their own village; and although no such compulsion exists in our own society, the prospect of marriage quite often necessitates some amount of migratory movement. Too, maintaining marital or family ties is a chief inducement for the wife and children when a family head decides to migrate.

Freedom from persecution has also been an important motive among many religious and racial minorities, as well as for intellectuals. Examples of mass movements of religious or racial minorities include the Puritan settlement of New England, the Jewish migration to Israel, the movement of American blacks out of the South, and the aforementioned interchange of Moslem and Hindu populations between India and Pakistan. Although the desire for intellectual freedom has never resulted in mass migration, some migrations of intellectuals have had important consequences. For example, persecution of intellectuals in Nazi Germany brought to the United States a group of famous scientists whose wartime contributions helped to hasten the Nazis' downfall.

A very common cause of intracounty movement is the desire for more adequate housing.[25] This motive is also the cause of intercounty migration, particularly when the suburbs of a metropolitan area are situated in a different county from its central city.

But migration also creates negative values. A major barrier to migration is that it involves a disruption of interpersonal relationships with kin and old friends. The farther the distance traveled, the greater this disruption, since return visits and contacts become more costly. The importance of this disruption can be measured by the fact that many migrants travel to the same towns or city neighborhoods to which relatives or other people from their town of origin have previously migrated. In addition, the volume of migration from one specific place to another tends to rise once a small nucleus of persons from the place of origin has established itself in the place of destination. The increasing volume of the migratory stream, once a nucleus of persons related in some way has been established, has been termed "chain migration." [26]

If migration involves movement to a new culture, deprivations may

25. Peter H. Rossi, *Why Families Move: A Study in the Social Psychology of Urban Residential Mobility* (Glencoe, Ill.: The Free Press, 1955).

26. John S. MacDonald and Leatrice D. MacDonald, "Chain Migration, Ethnic Neighborhood Formation, and Social Networks," *Milbank Memorial Fund Quarterly* (January, 1964), 52:1, 82–97. See also Oscar Handlin, *The Uprooted* (Boston, Mass.: Little, Brown, 1951), and Morton Rubin, "Migration Patterns of Negroes from a Rural Northeastern Mississippi Community," *Social Forces* (October, 1960), 39:1, 59–66.

also be caused by the necessity to discard old customs and learn new ones, and perhaps even a new language.

Laws restraining the entry or departure of international migrants are of course a very important deterrent to international migration, since very few persons are willing to pay the possible penalties involved in illegal entry or departure. It is true that, in defiance of their own government, a few East Germans have successfully scaled the Berlin wall and escaped to West Germany, and that an unknown number of Mexicans have illegally entered the United States. As a rule, however, relatively few persons ever attempt to disobey laws regarding international migrants, mainly because they are usually easy to enforce.

Most nations are permissive with respect to internal migration. A salient exception in recent years was the Soviet Union under Stalin. However, even then the Soviet government did not have complete success in enforcing its strictures prescribing and proscribing internal movements.

We may now discuss how the price system affects the volume of migration. The price system describes the expenditure of resources which is both a precondition to and a concomitant of migration. For many migrants the price of migration is in large part simply the monetary expense of moving. For self-employed persons it may also include the expenditure of savings in order to sustain a customary living-standard while building up a new business or practice. Since the cost of migration generally varies in direct proportion to the distance traveled, the number of migrants to a given place tends to vary inversely with the distance.

The total resources available for all goals also affects the decision to migrate. If the only drawback to migration is the expense of the move, then an increase in monetary income should increase the probability of migration. The secular increase in monetary income during the last century or more in the developed nations should have increased rates of migration, provided that the value and price of migration had remained constant. The fact that age-specific migration rates have been almost constant in the United States since 1947 may be an indication that the net value of migration is declining. In particular, the incentive of a better job is probably decreasing in importance, since regional disparities in income are being reduced.[27]

CONSEQUENCES OF MIGRATION

We shall now examine the possible consequences of migration for the individual, the area of net out-migration, the area of net in-migration,

---

27. U.S. Bureau of the Census, *Statistical Abstract of the United States, 1972* (Washington, D.C.: Government Printing Office), 1972, p. 319.

and the larger social system which includes areas of net in-migration and net out-migration. Our discussion must of course be in part speculative, since knowledge about these topics is still incomplete.

Before his move, the migrant doubtless will have anticipated a net balance of favorable consequences for himself. Sometimes, however, reality will fall short of his expectations, and dissatisfaction will provoke him to move either to his place of origin or to some other place. Grounds for presuming that many migrants will have considerable difficulty in adjusting themselves to their new environment are provided by studies which show, for instance, that migrants have a higher rate of mental disease than nonmigrants in the place of destination, even when other relevant differences between the two groups have been controlled.[28]

Net out-migration may have several important consequences for an area. It may relieve population pressure and cause the average level of wage and salary income to rise. The resultant rise in income may have a further effect on the area's mortality and fertility. On the other hand, net out-migration may cause the value of land and real estate to decline. Moreover, areas of net out-migration suffer the loss of the investments made to raise and educate children who spend their productive years elsewhere. Since migration rates are selective by age, areas of net out-migration often have few young adults relative to the number of children and aged persons. Certain of these areas may also lose their most intelligent or best educated persons in addition to their most rebellious and nonconforming elements—and for these reasons become unduly conservative.

Net in-migration may also have important consequences. If the area is definitely underpopulated, the resultant population increase may help the area to achieve *economics of scale* (reduction in the cost of goods obtainable by increasing the scale of production and of marketing) and thus raise the general standard of living. Under other circumstances, net in-migration may result in some decline in average wage and salary income. In either case, a net flow of in-migrants will tend to raise the price of land and real estate.

Generally, areas of net in-migration will have a rather high proportion of young adults. They will many times also have a rather heterogeneous and unconforming population, since in-migrants often come from diverse cultural backgrounds. For these reasons, areas of net in-

28. Everett S. Lee, "Socio-Economic and Migration Differentials in Mental Disease, New York State, 1949–1951," *Milbank Memorial Fund Quarterly* (July, 1963), 61:3, 249–68; and Judith Lazarus et al., "Migration Differentials in Mental Disease: State Patterns in First Admissions to Mental Hospitals for All Disorders and for Schizophrenia, New York, Ohio, and California, as of 1950," *Milbank Memorial Fund Quarterly* (January, 1963), 61:1, 25–42. See also Mildred B. Kantor, ed., *Mobility and Mental Health* (Springfield, Ill.: Charles C Thomas, 1965).

migration are often more tolerant of new ideas than are other types of area. It is also possible, however, that a high rate of in-migration fosters social disorganization, or *anomie*. Elizabeth Bott's concepts of *open* and *closed social networks* are useful tools in providing a rationale for this hypothesis. In a closed network a high proportion of a given person's acquaintances know one another; in an open network this is not so. Thus, group solidarity is presumed to be much higher when networks are closed. In the case of a sample of urban English families, Bott showed that open networks were characteristic of individuals who had recently moved into a community, and closed networks were typical of the community's oldtimers. It is also plausible to presume that open networks are more common among non-migrants in areas of heavy in-migration than in other types of areas simply because many of one's neighbors are often new.

Bott suggests that the type of network may affect the husband-wife relationship. Since a too-intense emotional load may disrupt a marriage, a closed social network, in which both husband and wife can seek understanding and companionship not only from the spouse but from many other persons as well, may aid marital stability.[29] This type of network, by strengthening informal social controls, may also be of aid in reducing crime and, by preventing loneliness, may even help to minimize rates of personal pathology. It is perhaps not coincidental that in California, where more than half the population is born out of the state, rates of marital disruption, of most forms of crime, and of suicide all appear to be substantially higher than for the United States as a whole.[30]

For the system comprising both the areas of net inflow and of net outflow, the direct effect of migration is of course to promote a redistribution of population. If migrants have been responsive to differences in job opportunities, this redistribution will further the economic development of the total system. The shift may either increase or decrease the homogeneity of the various subregions with respect to population density. In the United States the recent trend has been toward greater heterogeneity in population density among the small groupings of counties known as State Economic Areas. Moreover, between 1960 and 1970 nearly half the counties lost population although the total population

29. Elizabeth Bott, *Family and Social Network* (London: Tavistock Publications, 1957).

30. For the relevant data, see U.S. Bureau of the Census, *Census of Population, 1970*, Final Report PC(1)-D1, pp. 640–51 and Final Report PC(1)-D6, pp. 1298–99; *Statistical Abstract of the United States, 1972*, p. 144; and U.S. Public Health Service, *Vital Statistics of the United States, 1967*, Vol. 2, Part A (Washington, D.C.: Government Printing Office, 1969), p. 1–39.

increase was 24 million persons.[31] However, in other respects migration appears to foster regional homogeneity. Since migrants tend to move from low-income areas toward high-income areas, an important effect is to reduce regional income inequalities. This has been a noteworthy consequence of internal migration in the United States, where the southern states, with low per-capita income and high rates of net out-migration, have gradually come closer to the average income in the rest of the nation. Moreover, migration often helps to reduce regional disparities in other population characteristics as well. Migration of blacks away from the South has gone far toward making the regions of the United States less disparate in racial composition. Consequently, the locus of the problem of black-white relations has broadened to include the entire nation. Migration may also be diluting the Catholic and Jewish concentrations in the northeastern states and the Protestant predominance in the South and West, creating greater similarity between these regions in modes of interreligious accommodations.

31. U.S. Bureau of the Census, *Census of Population, 1970*, Final Report PC(1)-A1, pp. 25, 42.

PART THREE
POPULATION AND SOCIAL STRUCTURE

CHAPTER 7
AGE-SEX COMPOSITION

DETERMINANTS
OF AGE-SEX COMPOSITION

A population's *age-sex composition*—that is, the number of males and females in each of its age-groups—is determined by two factors. The first
is the population's sex ratio at birth. (*Sex ratio* is defined as the number
of males divided by the number of females, times 100.) The second is
the population's past history of births, deaths, and migrations.

A visual representation of the age-sex composition of an actual
population is presented in figure 3, which shows the age-sex composition of the Soviet Union in January, 1959. Two notable features of
this graph are the small number of persons of both sexes 10 to 19
years old, and the very large deficit of males relative to females at ages
30 and over. This graph shows a very irregular age-sex distribution—
a phenomenon commonly the result either of sharp temporary variations in the birth rate or of sharp and temporary changes in death or
migration rates for particular age-sex groups. In the 1959 Soviet distribution, the small proportion of persons 10 to 19 years old was largely
the result of the large reduction in the birth rate which took place
during World War II, when most men were separated from their
families. The extreme deficit of males at age 30 and over in the Soviet
Union is the result of the very large losses of military men during
World War I, the Civil War of 1917–21, and World War II, and of
the severe repressions which occurred during the Stalinist era. In most
other nations, there is also some predominance of females at older ages,

since typically male mortality is somewhat higher than female. However, in most populations there are more males than females at the younger ages, despite somewhat higher male mortality, because the sex ratio at birth averages around 105.

We have considered the example of the Soviet Union wherein fluctuating birth and death rates have created an irregular age structure. If, on the other hand, fertility, mortality, and migration rates remain relatively constant over time, a more regular age structure results. Let us consider now the types of age structure which emerge when age-specific birth and death rates remain constant over long periods of time. Assume initially a closed population (that is, one with neither in-migration nor out-migration) of one sex only, in which the distribution by age may be of any sort. Beginning with such a population, if birth and death rates at each age remain constant over a sufficiently long period of time, there eventually results a population with a calculable and unchanging rate of growth and with a calculable and unchanging age composition.[1] Such a population, eventuating from the long-term continuation of a given set of age-specific birth and death rates, is called a *stable population*. (A particular subtype of the stable population is the *stationary population;* this is a stable population in which the birth rate is exactly equal to the death rate.) Although the stable population is a mathematical model to which no actual population ever conforms precisely, the model is very useful because many populations are close approximations to it.

Stable populations have a regular age composition. Examples of four types of stable population—each formed by pairing one of two typical peacetime patterns of mortality with one of two typical patterns of fertility—are illustrated in figure 4. Specifically, these four examples are derived by cross-classifying a mortality level with an expectation of life at birth either of 69 years or of 35 years with a fertility level in which the number of daughters per woman of completed fertility is either 1.5 or 3. In the first example, where fertility and mortality are both low, the number of persons in each age-group declines very gradually from the youngest to the oldest age-group. In the second example, where fertility is low but mortality high, the age distribution again slopes down gradually from the youngest age-groups to the oldest. In the third example, where fertility is high but mortality is low, the age distribution slopes down very rapidly from youngest age-groups to the oldest. In the final example where fertility and mortality are both high, the age distribution is again one of rapid decline from the youngest age-groups to the oldest.

1. A. J. Lotka, *Theorie Analytique des Associations Biologiques* (Paris: Hermann, 1939). See also Alvaro Lopez, *Problems in Stable Population Theory* (Princeton, N.J.: Office of Population Research, Princeton University, 1961).

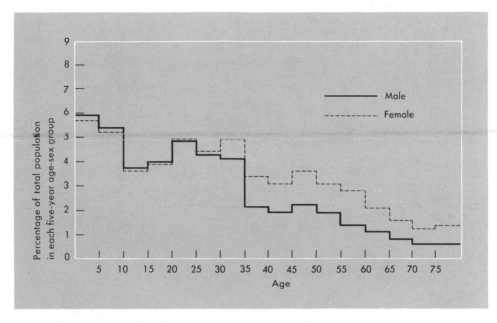

Figure 3 Age-Sex Structures of the Soviet Union, January, 1959. *Source:* James W. Brackett, "Projections of the Population of the USSR, by Age and Sex, 1964–1985," in U.S. Bureau of the Census, *International Population Reports*, Series P-91, No. 13 (Washington, D.C.: Government Printing Office, 1964), pp. 42–44.

These four examples illustrate an important generalization concerning stable populations—namely, that when fertility is high the proportion of the total population in the younger age-groups will be large without regard to the level of mortality, whereas when fertility is low the proportion of the population at young ages will be small, again without regard to the level of mortality.

This conclusion is at variance with much popular thinking. It is commonly assumed that populations with low mortality should have a high proportion of elderly persons, and populations with high mortality a low proportion. Now we see that it is difference in *fertility* rather than in mortality which is the chief cause of difference in age structure. Moreover, the small effect which mortality difference does exert on age structure is contrary to what might be expected, since a normal pattern of low mortality results in a slightly higher proportion of the very young than does a normal pattern of high mortality.

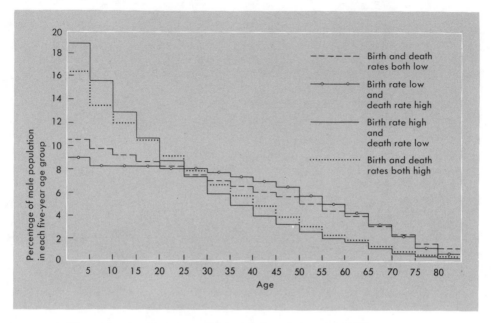

Figure 4   Age Structures of Stable Populations with Differing Birth- and Death-Rates. *Source:* Ansley J. Coale, *Regional Model Life Tables and Stable Populations* (Princeton, N.J.: Princeton University Press, 1966), pp. 184, 212 (mortality levels 8 and 22 cross-classified by Gross Production Rate 1.5 or 3 for West Model males).

CONSEQUENCES OF AGE-SEX COMPOSITION

We have seen from the example of the Soviet population that age distribution and the sex ratio at each age can be highly irregular. We have also seen that regular age distributions are frequently one of two types: one characterized by a *rapid* decline in number from the youngest to the oldest age-groups (we shall henceforth call this *a young population*), and the other characterized by a *gentle* decline (hereafter termed *an old population*). Variations in age-sex structure, whether of the regular or the irregular kind, may have various consequences for the society in which they occur. Let us now discuss some possible economic, demographic, familial, political, and psychological consequences of such variation.

Perhaps the most important of the economic consequences of differences in age structure is the effect of age structure on the dependency ratio. The *dependency ratio* is defined as the ratio of persons in dependent ages to persons in economically productive age-groups. The lower the ratio, the easier it is for persons in the economically productive ages to support those in the dependent age-group Although the terms *dependent ages* and *economically productive ages* can be variously defined, the definition we shall adopt here is that the dependent ages are the ages under 15 years and 65 years and over; the remaining age groups are economically productive.

What dependency ratio is associated with each of the four age structures shown in figure 4? The first age structure, generated by a pattern of low fertility and low mortality, has a dependency ratio of .607; the second, generated by low fertility and high mortality, has a ratio of .484; the third, generated by high fertility and low mortality, has a ratio of .985; and the last, generated by high fertility and high mortality, has a ratio of .796.

Thus, regardless of whether mortality is high or low, the young population created by high fertility has a much less favorable dependency ratio than the old population caused by low fertility. Moreover, high mortality, paired either with low or with high fertility, produces a slightly more favorable dependency ratio than low mortality similarly paired.

A second economic consequence of difference in age structure relates to the average age of the labor force. In the rapidly sloping age distribution caused by high fertility, the average age of persons within the broad age-group 15 to 64 years will be relatively young; in the gently sloping age structure caused by low fertility the average age will be relatively high. The average age of the labor force may have several consequences. A younger labor force has the advantage that its workers will be more flexible and able to learn new skills more readily. On the other hand, an older labor force is more responsible and experienced.[2] Further research on this topic would be valuable, since as yet we do not have exact knowledge of the magnitude of these various effects.

A third economic consequence of difference in age structure relates to the pattern of consumption. Societies with large proportions of children need to spend relatively large amounts of money on education; societies with larger proportions of elderly persons need to spend more on medical care. Changes in the age composition of a population may lead to changes in the patterns of consumption. For example, currently the United States is experiencing a decline in the total number of its

2.   Robert C. Atchley, *The Social Forces in Later Life: An Introduction to Social Gerontology* (Belmont, Calif.: Wadsworth, 1972), pp. 43–72.

children. As a consequence elementary school enrollment, which totalled about 34 million in 1970, fell to about 32 million by 1972.[3]

An irregular age structure may also have consequences with respect to the supply of labor, which will influence the wage and salary rate for particular age-groups. For example, in the early 1950s in the United States there were relatively few persons 20 to 29 years old, and starting salaries of persons of this age entering the labor force were exceptionally high. According to economist Richard Easterlin, the association between the scant supply of new entrants to the labor force during this period and their high wage and salary level was a causal rather than a coincidental relationship.[4] For the late 1960s and early 1970s an opposite situation obtained, since the number of young entrants to the labor force in the United States was then very large, tending to reduce the wage and salary level of this group.

Variation in age structure will also have demographic consequences. In particular, as noted in chapter 4, a young population will tend to have a much lower crude death-rate than an old population, since mortality is highest at advanced ages. For example, consider the two low-mortality populations illustrated in figure 4: the crude death-rate is 10 per thousand in the old population generated by low fertility, and only 5 per thousand in the young population caused by high fertility. This difference in crude death-rate occurs despite the fact that the death rates at each age are identical for both populations. It is also obvious that the crude birth-rate will be affected either by an abnormal sex ratio or by an unusually large or small proportion of persons of reproductive age. In the United States in the 1950s and early 1960s the crude birth-rate was depressed by the very small proportion of persons who were of reproductive age. Crude rates of migration are also affected by a population's age-sex structure. In particular, since young adults tend to be more mobile than middle-aged or elderly persons, a young population tends to have a higher migration rate than an older one.

Variations in age-sex structure affect the probabilities of marriage for men and women. If we assume that men usually marry women a few years younger than themselves, then the women in any population in which the age structure has a downward slope will have more difficulty in finding mates than will men. This is because there will be more women aged $x - n$ years than men aged x. The problem is of course accentuated for a young population with its very pronounced age-slope.

3. U.S. Bureau of the Census, *Current Population Reports*, Series P-20, No. 247 (February 1973).

4. Richard A. Easterlin, *The American Baby Boom in Historical Perspective*, Occasional Paper 79 (New York: National Bureau of Economic Research, 1962).

In societies with a young population but high mortality, a high proportion of women can marry, but only because a large number of men who have been widowed or divorced remarry women who have never married. However, in such a society a large proportion of the many widows and divorcees will never be able to remarry. On the other hand, in societies with a young population and low mortality, a substantial proportion of women can never marry since the combined supply of young men, widowers, and divorcees is not often sufficient to provide husbands for the large number of young women.

The excess loss of men in war causes additional difficulty for women seeking husbands. The shortage of eligible men can, it is true, be ameliorated through a decline in the age of male marriage, through increasing the proportion of men who will ever marry, or through selective inmigration of males. In countries suffering major losses of men through war, however, the proportion of women who never marry among cohorts of women slightly younger than the men who were of fighting age is usually considerably reduced.

A sudden change in the rate of population growth may also affect the sex ratio at marriageable ages and hence influence marriage probabilities. For example, after World War II the number of births in the United States increased quite suddenly over the number which had prevailed during the war. Since in the United States men marry at about age 23 to women who are on the average age 20 to 21, the marriage market for females is greatly influenced by the relative number of males who are two or three years older. In the United States there were slightly more boys born in 1941–43 than girls born in 1944–46. In contrast, the number of girls born in 1947–49 was 14 percent greater than the number of boys born in 1944–46.[5] Thus, girls born right after World War II and reaching marriageable age in the late 1960s had substantially poorer prospects for marriage than girls born during World War II, who reached marriageable age at mid-decade. However, it is also appropriate at this point to mention that an opposite situation existed in the early 1950s. At that time, because of the declining number of births during the late 1920s and early 1930s, chances for women to marry were excellent, but the chances for men relatively less satisfactory. Moreover, women born in the 1960s and early 1970s will also have excellent chances to marry in the 1980s and early 1990s.

Variations in marriage prospects may have further effects. For example, one may speculate that relatively poor marriage prospects may have influenced the self-image of American females born during the post-

5. U.S. Public Health Service, *Vital Statistics of the United States, 1963*, Vol. 1, *Natality* (Washington, D.C.: U.S. Government Printing Office, 1964), Sec. 1, p. 3.

war period, and that to preserve feelings of self-worth, many of them made a more favorable evaluation of an occupational career. We do know that a higher proportion of those coming of age in the late 1960s made a serious preparation for one of the higher professions than of those reaching maturity in the 1950s or early 1960s.[6] Moreover, the increasing interest among females in pursuing a career was no doubt a causal factor in the Women's Liberation Movement which burgeoned at this time.

Variations in the proportions of marriageable men to marriageable women also lead to variations in the rate of illegitimacy. In particular, wars which markedly reduce the sex ratio at young ages often cause a substantial rise in illegitimate births. For those nations which participated in World War II, a very high inverse correlation is obtained between the sex ratio among persons 15 to 49 years old in 1949, and the ratio of illegitimate to total births.[7]

Differences in age structure may even affect the relative power of liberals and conservatives within a nation. A higher proportion of all voters will be of advanced years in an older than in a younger population, and there is some tendency for persons to grow more conservative with age (although much of the observed difference in political party identification in the United States by age has resulted because persons who are now elderly were more apt to be Republican when they were young than are more recent cohorts of voters).[8]

It is well known that the morale of the aged is an important problem in the economically developed nations because it is difficult for many older citizens to find meaningful and important roles. If the developed nations had a younger population, the importance of this problem would of course be greatly diminished. However, these nations do *not* have younger populations, and so the problem must be faced in its full magnitude. Furthermore, since economic development and low fertility are very closely associated, it appears that the proportion of elderly persons in the developed nations will tend to remain quite high for some time to come.

6. U.S. Bureau of the Census, *Statistical Abstract of the United States, 1972* (Washington, D.C.: Government Printing Office, 1972), p. 134.

7. David M. Heer, *After Nuclear Attack: A Demographic Inquiry* (New York: Praeger, 1965), pp. 384–88.

8. Matilda W. Riley and Ann Foner, *Aging and Society*, Vol. I, *An Inventory of Research Findings* (New York: Russell Sage Foundation, 1968), p. 472.

CHAPTER 8
POPULATION GROWTH AND ECONOMIC DEVELOPMENT

THE GAP BETWEEN ECONOMICALLY DEVELOPED AND LESS DEVELOPED NATIONS

In the world today a great gulf divides the economically developed nations from the less developed. In 1958 the United States, with only 6 percent of the world's population, produced about 35 percent of the world's economic goods and services; the more developed nations, with only 32 percent of the world's population, produced *in toto* about 82 percent; the less developed nations, containing 68 percent of the world's population, produced a mere 18 percent. The extreme gap between the most developed and the least developed nations is illustrated by the per-capita product in the United States which was some thirty times higher than that in India or China.[1]

The contrast between the developed and less developed nations might be tolerable for the latter if they were completely isolated from the developed nations. Because of modern means of communication and transportation, however, the poorer nations are now more aware than ever of the economic performance of the wealthier nations. This awareness has incited the people and governments of the poorer nations to intensely desire rapid economic development. We see in this desire what has been called the "revolution of rising expectations."

---

1. Simon Kuznets, *Postwar Economic Growth* (Cambridge, Mass.: Harvard University Press, 1964), pp. 29–33.

In this chapter we shall discuss the role of population growth in stimulating and retarding economic development. We shall focus our discussion on the less developed nations. However, we shall also consider the effect of population growth rates on economic growth in the now-developed countries, particularly in those instances where population growth in a developed country may exert an influence opposite from that which it would exert in a poorer nation. We shall examine: (1) two contrasting effects of population growth on costs of production; (2) the effect of changes in population growth rates on the ratio of dependents to wage-earners; (3) the effect of population growth on the volume of productivity-stimulating investment; and (4) the possible effect of population growth on the motivation for economic development.

TWO EFFECTS OF POPULATION GROWTH ON COSTS OF PRODUCTION

Population growth has two contradictory effects on the cost of productive operations. One effect tends to reduce costs, the other to raise them.

As far back as 1776, Adam Smith, in his famous book *Inquiry into the Nature and Causes of the Wealth of Nations,* discussed *economies of scale* (how the cost of production could be reduced by increasing its scale).[2] Henry Ford demonstrated Adam Smith's principles by producing his Model T Ford at a price considerably lower than that charged by his competitors, who did not use mass-production techniques. That large-scale production is often less costly than small-scale production has now been proved in a myriad of instances. If population growth, by expanding the market for goods, allows for an increase in the scale of production, and if an increase in scale reduces average productive costs, then population increase will be a cause of lower production costs. For example, it is quite possible that the past increases in the population of the United States made possible certain economies of scale in American productive and service industries, perhaps particularly in railroad transportation and in heavy industry. Furthermore, currently, Australia and a few other nations with low population density might achieve lower avearge costs through the economies of scale made possible by a further increase in population. However, it should be recognized that there is probably an optimum scale of production and that increasing the scale of operations

---

2. Adam Smith, *Inquiry into the Nature and Causes of the Wealth of Nations* (New York: The Modern Library, 1937).

beyond a certain point results in higher rather than lower average costs. For example, the streets of American cities are now so overcrowded that there can be little doubt that the average cost of intraurban transport operations would be considerably reduced by a decline rather than by an increase in the scale of vehicular movement.

But a burgeoning population is not the only means by which an escalation of business operations can be achieved. International trade also holds great potential since a large international market may offer as many opportunities for economies of scale as a large internal market. Moreover, the internal market for all but the most necessary goods and services will increase as much through a rise in the nation's per-capita income as by an increase in the number of consumers.

The detrimental effect of population growth on the average cost of production is that every increase in population results in a diminution in natural resources per capita. This point was forcibly brought to the attention of the world by Malthus in his *Essay on Population*[3] and was strongly reiterated by David Ricardo, the most outstanding systematizer among the early nineteenth-century English classical economists. These early economists developed what is called *the law of diminishing marginal returns*. Their discussion revolved about the two factors of production: land and labor. Land, they held, was a fixed factor since the amount of land could in only small degree be altered through human intervention. Labor was a variable factor since each increase in population would result in a rise in the size of the labor force. The interest of the classical economists lay in (1) the total amount of food that could be produced on a given piece of land, depending on the amount of labor that was applied, and (2) the marginal increment in production that could be achieved by applying an additional unit of labor. According to their theory, at the very beginning, when the first few units of labor are applied, the marginal returns are increasing—that is, each successive unit of labor adds more units of product than its predecessor. Thus the classical economists recognized the economies of scale. However, beyond a certain point, they argued, further applications of labor would each earn successively less additional product, until finally an additional unit of labor would result in no marginal return at all.

Malthus contended that the world of his time was subject to diminishing marginal returns from additional increments of labor, and that any increase in population would result in a decline in economic production per capita. That Malthus proved wrong in his prediction of a

---

3. Thomas Robert Malthus, *Population: The First Essay* (Ann Arbor, Mich.: University of Michigan Press, 1959).

declining living standard was the result of the unforeseen advances in technology which have taken place since his time. There can be no doubt, however, of the overall validity of the classical analysis. As population increases, lands which were previously thought insufficiently productive are brought into use, minerals and fuels which were earlier thought to be too inaccessible or of insufficiently high quality are extracted, and more units of labor are applied to each unit of land or other resources. Under these conditions, and if we assume no advances in technology, living standards are bound to decline once the population exceeds a certain critical size.

What remains at issue is the exact size of population beyond which diminishing returns set in, and the exact relation between each increment in population size and each increment in production. Although this is, as it long has been, a subject for empirical investigation, the difficulties in finding a valid answer are about as great as ever, and so our knowledge in this regard is still very limited. We do know that at present the developed nations and particularly the United States, by far the richest of the major developed nations, have much superiority in natural resources per capita over the less developed nations. For example, in the mid-1950s the United States had about 1.14 hectares (1 hectare = 10,000 square meters, or 2.471 acres) of cultivated land per capita, compared to a world average of 0.49 hectares, 0.39 hectares in India, and 0.19 hectares in China.[4] The United States and most other developed nations also have a great advantage in the magnitude of their energy reserves (or energy potential) obtainable from coal, oil shale, petroleum, natural gas, fuelwood, and water power. In the mid-1950s, the United States possessed 72 million kilowatt-hours of energy potential per capita, the highest of any country in the world. The Soviet Union had 53 million, West Germany 37 million, and the United Kingdom 27 million. However, the world average was only 13 million kilowatt-hours, in China it was 4.5 million, and in India only 1.4 million. Moreover, 53 percent of the population of the world lived in nations with less than 1.9 million kilowatt-hours of energy potential per capita.[5]

Admittedly these data on resources are crude and imperfect. Nevertheless, their inexactness cannot hide the large disparity between nations in per-capita natural resources. From these data, it is obvious that any further population increase in the less developed nations will reduce their already minimal resource base.

4. Norton Ginsburg, *Atlas of Economic Development* (Chicago, Ill.: University of Chicago Press, 1961), pp. 46–47.

5. Ibid., pp. 58–59.

CHANGES IN THE RATE
OF POPULATION GROWTH
AND IN THE DEPENDENCY RATIO

In the previous chapter we discussed how different patterns of fertility and mortality produce differences in the dependency ratio. We pointed out that in stable populations high fertility has a major influence in creating an elevated dependency ratio, and that low mortality has a minor influence in the same direction. Stable populations with high fertility and low mortality therefore have the highest ratio of dependents to productive age-groups.

In their book *Population Growth and Economic Development in Low-Income Countries*, Ansley J. Coale and Edgar M. Hoover have prepared some very interesting projections of how changes in fertility and mortality might affect the ratio of non-earning dependents to earners in India.[6] According to their projection which assumed declining mortality but no change in fertility, the ratio of dependents to wage-earners would rise from 1.51 in 1956 (the actual figure) to 1.71 in 1986. On the other hand, according to the projection assuming the same decline in mortality but also a 50 percent decline in fertility by 1981, the ratio of dependents to wage-earners would have declined to 1.24 in 1986.[7] It is clear from these figures that the level of living in the average Indian family would be greatly improved by such a reduction in fertility, whereas continued decline in mortality might threaten existing living levels merely by increasing the number of persons dependent on each wage-earner.

POPULATION GROWTH
AND CAPITAL INVESTMENT

According to many economists, developed nations with a free-enterprise economy benefit from an acceleration of population growth because such an acceleration helps them avoid business depressions. According to Keynesian economic theory, business depression results when the amount of money which a population wishes to save is greater than that which potential investors wish to invest. It is contended that an

6. Ansley J. Coale and Edgar M. Hoover, *Population Growth and Economic Development in Low-Income Countries* (Princeton, N.J.: Princeton University Press, 1958).

7. Ibid., p. 235.

increase in the number of children per family will result in a reduction in intended savings, since an enlarged family will have greater consumption needs. It is further argued that increased population growth will result in larger intended investment because increased capital will be seen to be necessary to provide for the expected increase in total consumption. It is therefore concluded that a rise in fertility will either cure an existing depression or forestall a future one.[8] The "baby boom" in the United States in the years following World War II was thus welcomed by many economists and business spokesmen as a guarantee against severe depression. The argument advanced by these economists has merit, and it is quite possible that reductions in fertility in developed nations with a free-enterprise economy may have detrimental results unless governments act to ensure that consumption is increased in other directions.

A very different relation between population growth and capital investment obtains in the poor nations of the world. Relative to the developed nations, the less developed nations have on a per-capita basis very small amounts of capital. One of their major needs, therefore, is for additional investment. Capital is needed for highways, railroads, communication systems, electric-power generators, irrigation pumps, factories, and machinery. Equally needed is further investment in human beings. A literate populace is necessary even to apply existing technology; a still higher average level of education is necessary before a nation can adapt current technology to special local conditions; and a higher level yet before a nation can be instrumental in pioneering the development of new technology.

On the other hand, because the less developed nations are so short of it, added amounts of capital do more to raise productivity. Economists have estimated that for these nations a given amount of new capital investment will be associated with an increase in annual national income equal to approximately one-third the amount of the capital.[9] In the technical terms of the economist, the *incremental capital output ratio* for these nations would be said to be about 3.

How is this capital raised? Basically, the less developed nations can increase their capital in two ways. Either they must obtain funds from abroad by loan or gift, or they must obtain the money from within the economy by raising total income or by reducing total consumption. Many

8. For the fullest exposition of this argument see W. B. Reddaway, *The Economics of a Declining Population* (London: Allen & Unwin, 1939).

9. Ansley J. Coale and Edgar M. Hoover, *Population Growth and Economic Development in Low-Income Countries*, pp. 181–224. The magnitude of the incremental capital-output ratio will vary according to the broadness of one's definition of capital investment. The broader one's definition, the larger the magnitude of the incremental capital-output ratio.

of the less developed nations do not wish to become excessively indebted to developed nations, nor are the developed nations always anxious to give or lend capital. Therefore, the leadership groups of the less developed nations are usually very much concerned with increasing the level of investment in their nations through internal means.

How does a decline in population growth-rate achieved through fertility reduction affect the ability of a less developed nation to raise additional capital sums to increase its productivity? Two relationships are relevant. First, a decline in fertility will result in fewer dependents per wage-earner, and hence each wage-earner can be either motivated or forced to save a larger proportion of his total income.[10] These savings can then be used to increase the nation's investment in new factories, roads, schools, and so on. Secondly, any nation with a growing population must spend a certain proportion of its invested capital merely to provide the additional population with the same amount of capital equipment per person already enjoyed by the existing population. For example, a growing population will need additional housing, school buildings, hospitals, and factories. Hence, not all of the capital which a nation invests can be spent on capital improvements to increase per-capita productivity and raise the level of living. In sum: The higher the nation's rate of population growth, the greater the amount of capital that will be necessary merely to make provision for the added population, and therefore, the less will be the funds left over for making capital improvements to improve productivity.

Coale and Hoover complete their work by considering how their projected 50 percent decline in fertility might affect: (1) the total amount of capital investment; (2) the proportion of total capital investment applicable to improving productivity rather than providing for population increase; and (3) resultant increase in income per equivalent adult consumer.[11] They assume that 30 percent of any increase in income per equivalent adult consumer will be invested. They also assume that investments made merely to maintain the existing level of equipment per capita of an expanding population will not serve to raise total production—a reasonable assumption since during the period of their projection the size of the labor force will not be materially affected by fertility reduction. They do not assume any declining returns caused by increasing scarcity of natural resources per capita.

According to Coale and Hoover, in the population with declining

10. Governments force savings and investment through taxing the populace and using the proceeds for government-sponsored capital investment. This is the usual method fo financing investment in the Soviet Union and other Socialist nations.

11. In calculating the number of equivalent adult consumers, men 10 and over were given a weight of 1, children under 10 a weight of 0.5, and women 10 and over a weight of 0.9.

fertility, income per equivalent adult consumer would gradually rise relative to that in the population with unchanging fertility. After ten years (i.e., in 1966), average income per consumer in the population with declining fertility would be only 3 percent higher than in the population without fertility change. However, by 1976 it would be 14 percent higher, and by 1986, 41 percent higher. Assuming fertility reduction, income per consumer would be 95 percent higher in 1986 than it had been in 1956; assuming no fertility reduction, it would be only 38 percent higher.[12] All of these projections imply that fertility reduction would have a very substantial effect on the future course of economic development in India and other poor nations.

POPULATION GROWTH AND THE MOTIVATION FOR ECONOMIC DEVELOPMENT

Most of our previous discussion has pointed out various detrimental effects of a high rate of population growth, and particularly of a high birth rate, for economic development in the poorer nations. We shall now examine an argument that these various detrimental effects may be offset by the influence of a high rate of population growth in stimulating the motivation for improved productivity. The chief exponent of this argument has been the economist Albert Hirschman, who argues that the population pressure resulting from a high rate of population growth will lead to counterpressures designed to maintain or restore the nation's traditional level of living. This counter-pressure will take the form of increased motivation to undertake a new organization of economic activities based on a more advanced technology. Once a society has taken the crucial step of discarding traditional economic activity, it can then make the additional effort needed to increase the per-capita level of living, even despite the continuing growth in population.[13]

Hirschman's argument is of course very similar to that of Durkheim, which we discussed in chapter 1. It would be difficult to deny Hirschman's contention that productivity-increasing activities take place under conditions of rapid population growth. However, the crucial question for present-day policy-makers is whether a decline in the rate of population growth through fertility reduction in the now less-developed nations

---

12. Coale and Hoover, *Population Growth and Economic Development in Low-Income Countries*, p. 280.

13. Albert O. Hirschman, *The Strategy of Economic Development* (New Haven, Conn.: Yale University Press, 1958), pp. 176–82.

would bring about a reduction in their motivation to undertake productivity-increasing efforts. Hirschman has produced no empirical evidence to show that this would occur.[14] Moreover, it is at least plausible to argue that all of the poorer nations are now highly motivated in favor of economic advance simply because the difference between their own level of living and that in the developed countries has (as we have already seen) been made manifest by modern methods of communication and transportation. On the other hand, Hirschman's argument can be supported in part by the possibility that a reduction in mortality may have a very beneficial influence on motivation for increasing the productivity of economic activities, a point we considered in chapter 4.

Another argument, which claims that motivation in favor of increasing economic productivity may be endangered by programs of population control, is that of David McClelland. He argues that the supply of potential entrepreneurs—that is, persons with a high motivation to achieve innovations in economic activity—may be limited if a fertility-reduction campaign is accepted most eagerly by the middle socio-economc strata, wherein McClelland believes a disproportionate number of potential entrepreneurs are bred.[15] However, McClelland's caveat may be ignored as long as fertility-contrtol programs achieve acceptance from the lower social strata in greater proportion than from the middle and upper strata.

14. To the contrary, Hirschman even argues that the adoption of birth-control techniques may serve to teach a populace that the environment *can* be controlled and hence aid it in coping with the tasks of development. See Hirschman, *The Strategy of Economic Development*, pp. 180–81.

15. David C. McClelland, *The Achieving Society* (Princeton, N.J.: D. Van Nostrand, 1961), p. 424.

CHAPTER 9
POPULATION AND POLITICAL POWER

We may define the *political power* of a nation or group as the ability to influence other nations or groups to engage in policies which they would not otherwise undertake. This power may be exercised through: (1) providing rewards for compliance with one's goals; (2) threatening the use of force for failure to comply; and (3) the actual use of force when compliance has not otherwise been induced. Population variables influence the relative power both of nations in international politics and of groups engaged in political conflict within a nation. However, the influence of population variables on power is not always a simple one. In particular, it would be wrong to postulate that political potency can always be enhanced by an increase in population size. We shall presently discuss why this is so.

POPULATION AND POWER IN INTERNATIONAL AFFAIRS

Although there is without question a positive correlation between the size of a nation's population and the potency of its influence in international affairs (certainly none of the nations with a very small population is a great power), it is only a rough one. For instance, most persons would agree that the United States is the most powerful nation in the world, yet it is exceeded in population by China, India, and the Soviet Union. There would also be general agreement that the Soviet Union is the second most important power in the world, but the population of the USSR is less than that of either China or India. Perhaps the most striking recent illustration of the imperfect correlation between population size and power in international affairs was the 1967 victory of Israel, with only about 2.5 million population, over the Arab opponents whose combined population totaled about 100 million.

Clearly, population size alone cannot explain variations in international power. Probably five variables are necessary to explain a nation's force in world affairs: (1) *population size,* (2) *income per capita,* (3) the *possession of natural resources* specifically necessary *for warfare,* (4) the degree of *governmental motivation* to achieve international goals, and (5) the *efficiency* of government *in mobilizing resources* to attain these goals.[1]

Population size is important for two reasons. First, a large population is necessary if a nation is to have a large body of men in military service. Secondly, it is important because from the productive effort of each member of the labor force a certain amount can be siphoned off to pay for the cost of a military establishment, foreign aid, and other expenditures which enhance the power of the nation. If this amount is constant for each member of the labor force, then the effort which can be expended to maintain or increase the nation's power will vary directly with the size of the labor force. Moreover, the larger the population the larger the labor force, and hence, under the condition stated above, the potential resources available for increasing the nation's power will vary directly with the size of the nation's population.

The amount of productive effort which may be extracted from each member of the labor force and devoted to aggrandizing the nation's power may not, however, be constant, and income per capita is thus an important variable in explaining variation in national power. The higher the per-capita income, the lower will be the proportion of all income which must be spent on the absolute necessities of life. Hence, the proportion of each individual's income which can be spent to increase the power of the nation will vary directly with the level of per-capita income.

A nation will have greater military power to the extent that it possesses on its own soil the resources such as petroleum, coal, and iron ore which are specifically necessary for maintaining a military establishment.

Nonetheless, a nation which is potentially powerful because of a large population, high per-capita income, and requisite natural resources is not actually powerful unless it uses its potential resources efficiently. Nations with governments both highly motivated to exercise power in

---

1. In this exposition I am following closely (but not exactly) the thinking in Kingsley Davis, "The Demographic Foundations of National Power,'" in Morroe Berger et al., eds. *Freedom and, Control in Modern Society* (New York: Van Nostrand, 1954), pp. 206–43, and Katherine Organski and A. F. K. Organski, *Population and World Power* (New York: Alfred A. Knopf, 1961).

international affairs and skilled at doing so will have an advantage over nations which are either less highly motivated or unskillful in using the resources they have mobilized.

Table 5 shows the twelve nations having the largest population, the highest per-capita income, and (by way of a ranking of productive capacity) the greatest total production of steel. It is apparent from this table that population size and per-capita income are not well correlated: of the twelve nations of largest population, only the United States and West Germany are included in the dozen having the highest per-capita income.

Of the available single indicators of national power, aggregate steel production may be the most valid (although not invariably accurate). A high level of steel production obtains only when population is large and per-capita income is reasonably high. Moreover, the level of steel production is also somewhat dependent on governmental motivation in favor of international power, since a sizeable steel industry is a pre-requisite for large-scale armaments manufacture. In terms of total steel production, the United States in 1970 was the most important world power; the Soviet Union ranked second. Although these two nations were among the top four in total population, of the top twelve nations in population, only six would rank among the top dozen in power, as-

Table 5   The Twelve Nations with Largest Population, Highest Per-capita Income, and Greatest Steel Production, circa 1970

NATION	1972 POPULATION (IN MILLIONS)	NATION	1970 PER-CAPITA GROSS DOMESTIC PRODUCT (IN $)	NATION	1970 STEEL PRODUCTION (IN THOUSANDS OF METRIC TONS)
China	786	USA	4,734	USA	119,308
India	585	Kuwait	4,189	USSR	115,889
USSR	248	Sweden	4,055	Japan	93,322
USA	209	Canada	3,676	West Germany	45,040
Indonesia	129	Denmark	3,141	United Kingdom	28,316
Japan	106	Switzerland	3,135	France	23,773
Brazil	98	West Germany	3,034	Italy	17,277
Bangladesh	80	Luxembourg	2,960	China	17,000
Pakistan	67	Norway	2,944	Belgium	12,611
West Germany	59	Australia	2,916	Poland	11,480
Nigeria	58	France	2,901	Czechoslovakia	11,480
United Kingdom	57	Belgium	2,633	Canada	11,200

Sources: Population: Population Reference Bureau, *1972 World Population Data Sheet* (Washington, D.C.: 1972); Per-capita Gross Domestic Product: *United Nations, Yearbook of National Account Statistics, 1971* (New York, 1973), Vol. 3, pp. 3–7; Steel Production: *United Nations, Statistical Yearbook, 1971* (New York, 1973) p. 288.

suming steel production to be an accurate indicator thereof. Hence, population size and power are apparently only roughly correlated.

If population size and political power are not highly correlated, it follows that a nation which wishes to increase its power relative to other nations should not necessarily encourage an acceleration of its population growth. There are two reasons why an acceleration of population growth may not augment a nation's power. First, an increased growth-rate made possible by a rise in fertility can produce additional military manpower only after a lag of some twenty years following the birth-rate rise. Secondly, a high rate of population growth may be very detrimental to the nation's ability to raise its per-capita income. For nations such as China, India, Bangladesh, Pakistan, and Indonesia, wherein the level of per-capita income is exceedingly low, the best method of increasing national power may be to curb population growth drastically and thereby facilitate the rise of per-capita income. On the other hand, nations such as the United States, with very high per-capita income, might suffer a decline in power if their population, relative to that of other nations, were to be considerably reduced.

Although an acceleration of population growth may not always be an optimum strategy for increasing national power, most governments have in the past assumed that it is. Sometimes this policy may have been justified. For example, the French government, stung by vanquishment in the Prussian War of 1870 and near defeat in World War I, resolved to increase the French birth rate to match that of Germany and instituted a system of financial aid to families.[2] Under other conditions, pro-natalist policies may be unwise. For example, Stalin prohibited legal abortion in the Soviet Union in 1936, probably because he was afraid of Hitler's armies and wished to raise the birth rate to provide more military manpower. Following the prohibition of abortion, the birth rate did rise. However, this increase in the birth rate probably lowered the proportion of women in the labor force and no doubt reduced the funds which could have been spent in expanding heavy industry. Moreover, the additional male babies born because abortion had been prohibited provided no increase in military manpower to repel Hitler's invasion in 1941.

POPULATION AND INTRANATIONAL POWER

In a democracy where one man has one vote it would seem obvious that groups with large populations would have more power than groups

2. David V. Glass, *Population Policies and Movements in Europe* (Oxford: Clarendon Press, 1940), Chs. 3 and 4, and Joseph J. Spengler, *France Faces Depopulation* (Durham, N.C.: Duke University Press, 1938).

with a small number. Certainly many minority racial, religious, and ethnic groups have often assumed that they could relieve themselves of persecution if only they could increase their number sufficiently to gain greater voting power. In the United States it has been suggested that elements within the Roman Catholic Church may have encouraged large families among Catholic parishioners in order to gain the Church greater political strength and counter Protestant-sponsored policies considered inimical to the Catholic interest.[3]

In many cases a larger population *has* provided the minority group with an increase in political power. In the early days of the United States, Roman Catholics suffered a great deal of political persecution at the hands of the overwhelming majority of Protestants. As their numbers increased, the Catholics found themselves in an ever more favorable political position, and in 1960 one of their number, John F. Kennedy, finally was elected President. The tremendous increase in the proportion of Catholics in the total U.S. population over the past 100 years has been caused by both very heavy immigration from abroad and a somewhat higher Catholic birth rate than that of the rest of the nation's population.

The relation between the two trends we have just discussed is probably one of cause and effect. However, an increase in population is not the only road to greater power for a minority group. The case of the American Jewish group is instructive. Jewish fertility has been less than that of any other religious group in the United States. On the other hand, individual Jews have made great strides in advancing their socio-economic status, so that at present American Jews have a higher average income and a generally higher occupational and educational status, than either Catholics or Protestants.[4] In all probability, Jews have increased potency in the United States not through an increase in number (currently they constitute only about 3 per cent of the population[5]) but because so many individual Jews have gained influential positions in the society.

It is interesting to note, moreover, that American blacks are most persecuted where they form the largest proportion of the population. From the standpoint of civil rights, the relative position of the American black is at its worst in Mississippi, Alabama, and the other Deep South states wherein blacks form a relatively large proportion of the total popu-

3. For a discussion of Roman Catholic encouragement of large families see Judith Blake, "The Americanization of Catholic Reproductive Ideals," *Population Studies* (July, 1966), 20:1, 27–43.

4. Sidney Goldstein, "Socioeconomic Differentials among Religious Groups in the United States," *American Journal of Sociology* (May 1969) 74:6, 612–31.

5. U.S. Bureau of the Census, *Current Population Reports*, Series P-20, No. 79 (2 February 1958), p. 6.

lation, and at its best in those northern and western states with relatively small black populations. A major reason for this situation may be the fact that the socio-economic status of individual blacks is so low in the Deep South. The principle of "one man, one vote" is meaningless in states where blacks can be kept from the polls by economic threats. Moreover, the vote alone will not mean power unless blacks have enough education to understand their own interests and sufficient finances to voice their views effectively. If American blacks wish to achieve a greater measure of power, their optimum population policy may be the encouragement of small families to allow close attention to the education and upbringing of each child. In this way blacks may raise their socio-economic status more rapidly, and through the attainment of higher status gain a large share in forming national, state, and local policies.

CHAPTER 10
POPULATION
LEGISLATION
AND POLICY

Change in population size, geographic distribution, composition, and process may all be influenced by governmental decrees and legislation. Some of the legislation affecting population is intentionally designed to influence one or more aspects of a nation's population. However, much of the legislation affecting population has some other goal as its primary aim. Only the former can be called population policy, but we cannot neglect the latter since its total effect on population may be even greater than that of the legislation consciously designed to have an impact on population.

The ultimate *effect* of population legislation may be on size, geographic distribution, or composition. The *mechanism* to achieve any one of these effects is a change in one of the three population processes: mortality, fertility, and migration. Any legislation affecting a population process will of course have an impact on the rate of change in population size. In addition, laws which induce change in mortality, fertility, or migration differentials will also affect population distribution and composition. It will therefore be convenient to divide our discussion of legislation according to whether there is an attempt to influence mortality, fertility, or migration.

LEGISLATION AFFECTING MORTALITY

Although governments generally place a high value on the preservation of human life, they have other values to consider, and these sometimes take precedence over the maximum preservation of life. For example, almost all governments place the independence of the nation above the protection of human life, and many have also considered imperial aggrandizement to be a higher value. As a result, throughout human history wars and armed conflict have resulted in millions of deaths not only to fighting men but to civilians as well. Mankind has increasingly felt the inhumanity of war, however, and in the twentieth century has attempted to control its outbreak through the mechanism of international organizations. The first such organization, the League of Nations, was not successful in preventing World War II—mainly because it was not taken seriously by many of its member nations, and partly because the U.S. refused to join it. The second international organization, the United Nations, has enjoyed a qualified success. That is, since its inception following World War II, it has been able to help stave off encounters among various great powers but has failed to prevent a rash of smaller but very serious conflicts.

Almost all nations have attempted to reduce mortality among their own people by means of public health programs. These are measures for environmental sanitation, inoculation against infectious disease, and regulation of foods, drugs, and sanitary facilities. Although these measures cost relatively little money, their impact on mortality has been extremely great.

Many of the developed nations, including Great Britain, France, West Germany, Austria, Sweden, the Soviet Union, Australia, and New Zealand have also instituted governmental programs of medical care. In these nations either the government establishes medical clinics which provide the public with largely free care, or it makes a large contribution to the payment of patients' medical and hospital bills.[1]

Unlike most of the other developed nations, the United States does not have a general governmental program of free or subsidized medical care. Nevertheless, gradually the federal government has been assuming more and more responsibility in this area. Since 1946, the federal government, under the Hill-Burton Act, has subsidized the construction of hospitals, and for a long period it has appropriated large amounts of money for medical research. In 1965 Congress passed an amendment to the Social Security Act with two very important titles relevant to federal participation in medical care programs. Title 18 provides for the establishment of the *Medicare* program, whereby the hospital and medical

---

1. For a cross-national description of state-operated or state-subsidized medical care programs, see Matthew Lynch and Stanley Raphael, *Medicine and the State* (Springfield, Ill.: Charles C. Thomas, 1963), and Helmut Schoeck, ed., *Financing Medical Care: An Appraisal of Foreign Programs* (Caldwell, Idaho: Caxton Printers, 1962).

expenses of all persons 65 years old and over are in large part "covered" by the federal government. Title 19 establishes the *Medicaid* program, under whose terms each state, with the help of federal financing, is to provide free medical care for persons established as medically indigent according to a means test. This 1965 legislation obligates the federal government to large expenses for medical care without imposing a pattern of extensive government controls over the actual rendering of medical services.[2]

Government expenditures on health programs have probably had two principal effects on differential mortality. In the first place, they may have done more to reduce death rates among infants and children than among older adults. Thus their direct effect has probably been to cause the total population to be somewhat younger. The second probable effect has been to reduce social-class differentials in mortality. Since poor persons cannot generally afford adequate medical care, governmental programs of medical care probably do more to reduce death rates among the poor than among the well-to-do.

LEGISLATION AFFECTING FERTILITY

Legislation with a conscious attempt to influence fertility is of very long standing, and until recent times almost all of it was pro-natalist. The Code of Hammurabi, enacted in the twentieth century B.C. in Babylon, is the first recorded attempt to elevate fertility by means of legislation.[3] Pro-natalist policies were also enacted in Rome during the reign of Caesar Augustus, somewhere between 18 B.C. and 9 A.D. The *Lex Papia et Poppaea*, for instance, contained various provisions designed to encourage marriage and the raising of children: fathers were given preference in public office according to the number of children in the family, and mothers of large families were given the right to wear distinctive clothes and ornaments. According to Glass, the main intent of the laws was to encourage births not in the general population but rather among the aristocrats, who apparently were not reproducing themselves in sufficient numbers to please the government. However, the aristocrats chose not to let the government order their conjugal behavior, and the laws proved both unenforceable and ineffectual. They were abolished

2. For a detailed description of the Medicare and Medicaid programs see Arthur E. Hess, "Medicare: Its Meaning for Public Health," *American Journal of Public Health* (January, 1966), 56:1, 10–18, and Ellen Winston, "The New Medical Assistance Program," *Public Health Reports* (October, 1966), 81:10, 863–66.

3. David V. Glass, *Population Policies and Movements in Europe* (Oxford: Clarendon Press, 1940), p. 86.

entirely when Christianity, which placed a higher value on celibacy than on marriage, became the religion of Rome.[4]

Pro-natalist legislation was also enacted in France and in Spain during the seventeenth century. In Spain, men who married early or who had a large family received partial or full exemption from taxes. The French legislation was similar to the Spanish, but provided in addition that any of the nobility who had ten or more living legitimate children were henceforth to receive annual pensions. There is some doubt, however, whether the Spanish legislation was ever put into effect, and the French legislation was soon repealed.[5] The seventeenth-century Spanish and French pro-natalist policies had been established because, in the case of Spain, the government feared the military consequences of an absolute loss in population, and in the case of France, a loss relative to population in other nations. In Spain the population had declined from about 10 million in 1500 to about 6 million in 1700.[6]

During the eighteenth and early nineteenth centuries, the actual increase in European population largely stilled the demands for pro-natalist legislation. Pro-natalist sentiment revived in many European nations coincident with the fertility decline of the late nineteenth and early twentieth centuries. Pro-natalist legislation has probably been carried to its fullest extent in France, where, as previously mentioned, defeat by Prussia during the war of 1870 and the terrible losses of World War I caused the government to resolve that the French birth rate should match that of Germany. But such legislation has been important at one time or another in almost all of the European nations.

One of the principal components of modern pro-natalist legislation in France and other nations has been the program of family allowances. A *family-allowance program* may be defined as any program in which monetary payments are made to parents on behalf of their children without regard to individual financial need. According to this definition, many other nations beside France have such programs, including Australia, Austria, Belgium, Brazil, Bulgaria, Canada, Chile, Czechoslovakia, Finland, the German Federal Republic (West Germany), Great Britain, Hungary, Iceland, Ireland, Italy, Lebanon, Luxembourg, the Netherlands, New Zealand, Norway, Poland, Portugal, Romania, Spain, Sweden, Switzerland, the Union of South Africa, Uruguay, the USSR, and Yugoslavia.[7]

4. Ibid., pp. 86–90.

5. Ibid., pp. 91–95.

6. United Nations Department of Social Affairs, *The Determinants and Consequences of Population Trends* (New York: United Nations, 1953), p. 9.

7. James C. Vadakin, *Family Allowances: An Analysis of their Development and Implication* (Miami, Fla.: The University of Miami Press, 1958), pp. 41–46.

The French family-allowance system evolved gradually. Beginning in 1918, family-allowance schemes were voluntarily organized by various industries; each company within the industry contributed to an industry-wide equalization fund, which in turn distributed the family-allowance payments. Legislation in 1932 nationalized the system of family-allowance payments, and according to the new French law all industrial employees were to be given cash allowances for each dependent child. In 1939 the French system was further enlarged to include workers in all occupations.[8] In 1961, family-allowance payments in France were equal to 5 percent of the total national income and were a substantially higher proportion of national income than the family-allowance payments in any other major nation.[9]

An increase in the birth rate was also the main object of family-allowance programs introduced into Germany by Hitler, into Italy by Mussolini, and into the Soviet Union by Stalin. In the Soviet Union a munificent program for families with three or more children was enacted in 1944. This legislation closely followed the staggering population losses which the nation had suffered during the first years of World War II. However, in 1948 the benefits were cut in half, and after that date the impact of the program was further diluted by the very substantial increase in the Soviet wage level. In 1944 the monthly payment to a family after the birth of the fifth child had been about 51 percent of the average wage, whereas in 1964 it was worth only 12 percent. It is obvious that the Soviet government was much less concerned about increasing its birth rate in 1964 than it was twenty years earlier.[10] Since 1964 many Soviet demographers have expressed renewed concern that the birth rate in the Soviet Union was too low. As of 1972, however, there had been no change in official policy with respect to the family allowance program.[11]

In many of the nations with family-allowance programs the main aim has been social welfare rather than population increase. Since the parents of large families often do not have enough income to provide adequately for their children, family-allowance payments help to equalize the position of children from large families. In Sweden, for example, the main purpose of the family-allowance program has unquestionably been that of social welfare.[12] Nevertheless, it is doubtful that intent makes any

8. Glass, *Population Policies and Movements in Europe*, pp. 99–124.

9. David M. Heer and Judith G. Bryden, "Family Allowances and Fertility in the Soviet Union," *Soviet Studies* (October, 1966), 18:2, 153–63.

10. Ibid.

11. David M. Heer, "Recent Developments in Soviet Population Policy," *Studies in Family Planning* (November, 1972), 3:11, p. 257–64.

12. Glass, *Population Policies and Movements in Europe*, pp. 312–38.

difference; family-allowance payments probably have much the same effect on fertility whether the intent is pro-natalist or the desire to foster child welfare.

Legislation restricting birth control may also help to raise fertility. The motivation for passing such legislation is often pro-natalist; on the other hand, a very important attitude sustaining such legislation is the belief that the free availability of birth-control information and devices encourages sexual promiscuity. In various nations laws have been passed restricting not only abortion but also contraception. Until 1967 the most restrictive legislation against contraception was in France. A law enacted in 1920 prescribed imprisonment for anyone engaging in birth-control propaganda, divulging means of birth control, or facilitating use of methods to prevent pregnancy. An important loophole was that the condom could be legally sold if the sale was for protection from venereal disease only. Nevertheless, the law placed severe limitations on the establishment of clinics whose specific aim was to foster family planning.[13] In the United States very restrictive birth-control legislation was in effect in Connecticut and Massachusetts as late as 1965 and 1966. Since 1966, dissemination of contraceptive information and the sale of contraceptive appliances have been legal throughout the nation.

Although abortion is still illegal under most circumstances in a very large number of nations, marked shifts in public attitudes have occurred in recent years in many countries resulting in dramatic liberalization of prohibitory legislation. In 1967 the English Parliament enacted new legislation allowing abortion on broad social indications.[14] Various American state legislatures enacted liberalized abortion legislation in the late 1960s and early 1970s; perhaps the most important of these legislative changes was in New York State allowing abortion by a licensed physician on any grounds within the first twenty-four weeks of pregnancy.[15] In congruence with the shift in public opinion on this issue, the U.S. Supreme Court ruled on January 22, 1973, in *Roe* vs. *Wade* that during the first trimester of pregnancy the decision to have an abortion must be left solely to a woman and her physician. After the first trimester the Court decreed that regulations "reasonably related to maternal health" were permissible (such as a regulation requiring that abortions be performed in a hospital). However, legislation prohibiting abortion was deemed constitutional only for the rare instances where the

13.   Ibid., pp. 159–62; "Rapport sur la Regulation de Naissances en France," *Population* (July–August, 1966), 21:4, 647–48.

14.   Daniel Callahan, *Abortion: Law, Choice and Morality* (New York: Macmillan, 1970) pp. 142–43.

15.   Association for the Study of Abortion, *ASA Newsletter* (Summer 1970), 5:2, 2–4.

fetus has capacity for life outside the mother's womb and the abortion was not necessary to preserve the mother's physical or mental health.[16]

In the United States and other nations there are many laws which probably have pro-natalist consequences even though their main intent is doubtless one of furthering welfare. In the United States perhaps the most important of this kind of legislation is the federal income-tax law. According to the law, single persons are subject to a higher tax-rate than most married persons, since married couples may average their income and each spouse pay a tax on this average income rather than on his own income. Furthermore, the law allows each taxpayer a $750 exemption for each of his dependent children. Finally, a substantial tax deduction is given to holders of a home mortgage, who may deduct from their taxable income the interest they pay. Since a large mortgage is more frequent among family heads with children than among other taxpayers, this provision may also have pro-natalist consequences. In the United States the income-tax laws of the various states also tend to favor family heads with children over other taxpayers. The selective-service law in the United States may also have had an impact on the birth rate, since fathers were declared to be draft-exempt.

Although legislation restricting fertility is of much more recent origin than its opposite, within the last few years such legislation has assumed very great importance in many areas of the world. An early example of anti-natalist legislation was a decree passed in 1712 in Württemberg (now part of West Germany) prohibiting marriage unless ability to support a family could be proven.[17] Nevertheless, anti-natalist legislation was of little general consequence until after World War II.

In the postwar period, Japan was the first nation seriously to undertake an anti-natalist policy. Following the devastation of the war, living standards in Japan had fallen to 52 percent of the prewar average. Furthermore, Japan had been stripped of her territorial possessions in Manchuria, Korea, Taiwan, and Micronesia, and as a result was forced to receive 6.6 million repatriates and demobilized soldiers from abroad. In 1949 the House of Representatives of the Japanese Diet expressed its official belief that means should be taken to reduce the birth rate. In the previous year Japan had legalized induced abortion for reasons of maternal health, provided the applicant received the approval of a local committee. In 1949, in accordance with the new anti-natalist policy, legislation was enacted to allow abortion for economic reasons. In 1952, a further amendment to the law allowed abortion at the discretion of only

16. "United States Supreme Court Issues Sweeping Decision on Abortion," in *Family Planning/Population Reporter* (February, 1973), 2:1, 1–5.

17. Glass, *Population Policies and Movements in Europe*, p. 98.

one doctor and authorized midwives and nurses to give guidance in conception control. As a result of these legal changes, the reported number of induced abortions increased greatly from less than 250,000 per year in 1949 to annual totals of more than one million in 1953 and later years. Since 1955 the number of abortions has declined as the proportion of population practicing contraception has increased, and in 1964 it was less than 900,000. Coincident with the legalization of abortion and the official encouragement of contraception, fertility in Japan declined dramatically. In 1947 the gross reproduction rate had been 2.20, but since 1957 the gross reproduction rate has averaged around 1.0 or slightly lower.[18]

In recent years many other nations, particularly in Asia, have developed family-planning programs. As of 1973 the nations of more than 10 million population which had family-planning programs included Afghanistan, Algeria, Bangladesh, Ceylon, Chile, Colombia, Egypt, India, Indonesia, Iran, Iraq, Kenya, Malaysia, Mexico, Morocco, Nepal, North Vietnam, Pakistan, the People's Republic of China, Philippines, the Republic of China (Taiwan), South Africa, South Korea, South Vietnam, Sudan, Tanzania, Thailand, Turkey, Uganda, the United States of America, and Venezuela.[19] Let us consider a few of the programs in detail.

Communist China has been markedly ambivalent about its fertility policy, vacillating several times with respect to whether it has wanted to discourage fertility. However, as of 1972 the Chinese government was attempting several anti-natalist measures, including the discouragement of early marriage, provision of facilities for contraception and sterilization, the legalization of abortion, and even the denial of additional rations to children in large families. The Chinese government has published no data concerning the effectiveness of any of these measures.[20]

The Indian government, as early as 1952, adopted a national policy

18. Minoru Muramatsu, ed., *Japan's Experience in Family Planning—Past and Present* (Tokyo: Family Planning Federation of Japan, 1967), pp. 27, 69, 83–101.

19. Dorothy Nortman, "Population and Family Planning Programs: A Factbook," *Reports on Population/Family Planning* (September, 1973), No. 2 (5th ed.); Calman J. Cohen, "Mexico Lays Base for Nationwide Family Planning Program," *Population Dynamics Quarterly* (Winter, 1973), 1:1, 2–4.

20. Leo A. Orleans, "The Population of Communist China," in Ronald Freedman, ed., *Population: The Vital Revolution* (New York: Doubleday, 1964), pp. 227–39; Irene B. Taeuber and Leo A. Orleans, "Mainland China," in Bernard Berelson, ed., *Family Planning and Population Programs* (Chicago, Ill.: University of Chicago Press, 1966), pp. 31–54; and John S. Aird, "Population Policy and Demographic Prospects in the People's Republic of China," in U.S. Congress, 92nd, *People's Republic of China: An Economic Assessment* (Washington, D.C.: Government Printing Office, 1972), pp. 220–331.

in favor of family planning—but little was actually done until the advent of India's Five Year Plan in 1961. Since 1961 the financial expenditures of the program have increased severalfold. The Indian program envisions the establishment of a family-planning unit headed by a female physician for each rural area of about 75,000 persons and each urban district of about 50,000. In each family-planning unit a "block extension educator" is supposed to organize educational meetings on family planning and work with voluntary family-planning workers. Auxiliary nurse-midwives connected with each unit are trained in family planning and are expected to provide advice to pregnant women and new mothers while carrying out their regular duties. The principal methods of birth control encouraged at these units are vasectomy, condom, and IUD insertion. In many of the Indian states a small bonus is granted to both men and women who consent to a sterilizing operation and to women who accept an IUD. Since 1966 there has been a sharp shift away from the IUD toward the male methods of vasectomy and condom. As of 1972, however, the family-planning program had not yet been fully implemented, and there was as yet no firm indication that the portion already implemented had had any substantial effect on fertility. But if the program's magnitude continues to increase at the same rate as in the recent past, before very long its impact will probably begin to increase correspondingly.[21]

The family-planning program in Taiwan has been one of the most successful of the recent contraceptive programs. An island-wide program with unofficial government backing was begun in 1964 following a local program conducted in the city of Taichung. Initially, the IUD was the only contraceptive made available. Physicians in private practice were provided with IUD's and were paid about 75¢ for each insertion, from funds accruing from the interest on counterpart loans from the U.S. Agency for International Development (AID). An additional 75¢ for IUD insertion had to be paid by the patient. In 1967 oral pills were added to the offerings of the government program and in 1970 the condom. Field workers in each local community promote family planning, and a limited use is made of the mass media for this purpose. By 1972 more than half the married women 15 to 44 years of age were estimated to be current users of contraception.[22] The program in Taiwan

21. United Nations Department of Economic and Social Affairs, *Report on the Family Planning Programme in India*, Report No. TAO/IND/48 (20 Feb. 1966); Stanley Johnson, *Life without Birth* (Boston: Little, Brown, 1970) pp. 173–224; and Nortman, "Population and Family Planning Programs."

22. *Family Planning in Taiwan, Republic of China, 1965–66* (Taichung: Taiwan Population Studies Center, 1966); Johnson, *Life Without Birth*, pp. 68–92; and S. M. Keeny, ed., "East Asia Review, 1972" *Studies in Family Planning* 4:5, 119.

has been accompanied by a significant decline in fertility. In 1963, the year before the program began, the total fertility rate was 5.4, but by 1971 it had declined to 3.7.[23]

During the decade of the 1960s the United States government altered its attitude toward family planning. In February, 1965, AID announced that it would henceforth entertain requests from foreign nations for technical assistance in family planning.[24] By fiscal year 1968, it was extending help to twenty-six nations and its total spending for family and population planning amounted to 34.7 million dollars.[25] This amount rapidly increased, and by fiscal 1971 AID funding in this area was 95.9 million dollars, an amount equal to more than 5 percent of all AID obligations.[26]

Although for a number of years various state and local health departments in the United States had offered family-planning services, until recently the federal government had given no specific support. It was not until January, 1966, that the United States Department of Health, Education, and Welfare proclaimed its willingness to make funds available to state and local agencies for this purpose.[27] It is probable that this federal subsidization of family-planning programs has had significant impact among the poorly educated, who tend to be inadequately informed about birth-control methods and particularly about the newer methods such as the oral contraceptive and the IUD.

Fertility policies, if successful, will have a major impact on the age composition of a nation. Pro-natalist policies will tend to produce a young population, and anti-natalist policies an older one.

Governmental programs to influence fertility probably affect social-class differences in fertility, too. One may speculate that family-allowance programs have their greatest impact among low-income groups since the supplement for child-rearing awarded to low-income families is a comparatively higher proportion of their total family income. Furthermore, it may be presumed that restrictive laws concerning birth control prob-

23. *1965 Taiwan Demographic Fact Book, Republic of China* (Taipei: Department of Civil Affairs, Taiwan Provincial Govt., 1966), pp. 226–27; *1971 Taiwan Demographic Fact Book, Republic of China* (Taipei: Ministry of Interior, Republic of China, 1972), p. 501.

24. "Statements on Population Policy," *Studies in Family Planning*, No. 16 pp. 8–9.

25. *Population Program Assistance* (Washington, D.C.: Agency for International Development, 1969).

26. Phyllis Tilson Piotrow, *World Population Crisis: The United States Response* (New York: Praeger, 1973), p. 178.

27. "Statements on Population Policy," p. 8.

ably have their greatest effect in low-income groups, since married couples of higher socio-economic status can probably more easily evade them. Thus, consistent pro-natalist policies may encourage fertility among the lower socio-economic strata more than they do in the higher. On the other hand, anti-natalist programs which advertise the availability of birth-control devices and which subsidize their cost may ultimately discourage fertility within the lower strata to a greater extent than within the upper strata. Because of the possibility of this differential impact by social class, government legislation concerning fertility may greatly influence the genetic composition of a population. Further research to quantify this apparent effect will be of great value.

LEGISLATION AFFECTING MIGRATION

Migration legislation runs a very wide gamut. Laws concerning international immigrants and emigrants vary from complete prohibition to positive encouragement. Although in general the laws of most nations concerning internal migration are permissive rather than either prohibitory or encouraging, in certain countries governmental control over internal migrants has been vigorously exercised.

In the seventeenth and eighteenth centuries a mercantilist ideology, which saw a large population as the key to national wealth and power, encouraged many of the governments of Europe to attempt to prohibit emigration and to encourage immigration. In the late seventeenth century, the French Minister Colbert enacted legislation prescribing the death penalty for persons attempting to emigrate or helping others to emigrate anywhere except to a French colony. In 1721, Prussia passed a similar law, and the Prussian Emperor Frederick the Great invested state funds to subsidize the settlement of immigrants. In Russia both Tsar Peter and Tsarina Catherine subsidized colonists from abroad—mostly from Germany.[28]

The nineteenth century, influenced by the economic doctrines of *laissez faire*, was the great period of unrestricted international migration. During this century the European governments freely permitted emigration, and the newly independent United States of America welcomed millions of immigrants.

After World War I, governments again took a more active role in policy relating to international migration. The major events in this connection were the changes in U.S. immigration laws in 1921 and 1924 which greatly restricted the number of immigrants to the United States,

28. Glass, *Population Policies and Movements in Europe*, pp. 94–96.

establishing a quota for each of the countries outside the Western Hemisphere. Furthermore, each of the nations of northwest Europe was given a much larger quota relative to its population than those of southern or eastern Europe. This was done even though in the immediately preceding years rates of emigration from southern and eastern Europe had been much higher than from northwest Europe. The justification made at the time for the quota differentials was the presumed greater ease with which immigrants from northwest Europe could assimilate themselves.[29]

By the 1960s, a changing climate of opinion with respect to the inferiority or superiority of different ethnic groups made it possible for President Kennedy to advocate the abolition of the discriminatory national-origins quota system, and a law accomplishing this was enacted in 1965 under the Johnson administration. The 1965 law called for the abolition of the national-origins quota system as of July 1, 1968—but nevertheless imposed an overall annual quota of 170,000 immigrants from outside the Western Hemisphere and 120,000 from within it (exclusive of immediate relatives of United States citizens). This legislation grants preference to persons with relatives already in the United States, to persons with needed occupational skills, and to refugees.[30]

Some nations, while placing severe restrictions on immigrants in general, make use of positive inducements to encourage immigration from *selected* nations or groups. Australia, for example, has a national policy of attempting to attract an annual number of a certain type of immigrant equal to 1 percent of her total population. In many cases she even subsidizes their cost of transport. Since she maintains very tight restriction against immigrants from Asia, most of her new population comes from Europe.[31] Canada also subsidizes some new immigrants—for example, from the Netherlands—while placing severe restrictions on the immigration of nonwhites.[32] A similar policy of subsidizing selected immigrants only is in effect in Israel, which has committed itself to encouraging the immigration of Jews from anywhere in the world.

Restrictions against emigration are currently exemplified in the

29. Helen F. Eckerson, "Immigration and National Origins," *The Annals of the American Academy of Political and Social Science* (September, 1966), 367, 4–14.

30. Edward M. Kennedy, "The Immigration Act of 1965," *The Annals of the American Academy of Political and Social Science* (September, 1966), 367, 137–49.

31. Anthony T. Bouscaren, *International Migrations Since 1945* (New York: Praeger, 1963), pp. 105–8, and R. T. Appleyard, "The Economics of Immigration into Australia," Paper No. WPC/WP/71, delivered at the United Nations World Population Conference, Belgrade, Yugoslavia, 1965.

32. Bouscaren, *International Migrations Since 1945*, pp. 141–44; and William Petersen, *The Politics of Population*, pp. 301–22.

Soviet Union. Except in rather special cases, citizens of that nation have not been allowed to establish residence abroad.[33] Although the restrictions apply to all citizens of the Soviet Union, they have been particularly disturbing to Soviet Jews wishing to emigrate to Israel. As of 1973 some, but not all, Soviet Jews were being allowed to leave.[34]

The USSR is also a prime example of a nation which has exerted considerable control over internal migration. Even though policy was greatly liberalized after Stalin's death, the government, being the principal employer, still is able to promote in-migration to certain areas (such as Siberia) both by positive inducements and by compulsion, and to restrict voluntary in-migration by limiting the number of job openings in other areas. In practice, however, the actual movement has not always coincided with that planned. For instance, many persons who go to Siberia, are able to return because managers of enterprises in Moscow, Leningrad, and other western areas often succeed in hiring a larger number of employees than have been assigned them according to the terms of the government's comprehensive plan for the geographic distribution of labor.[35]

Although the United States has neither legislative restrictions on internal migration nor subsidies to encourage it, various types of governmental actions influence the flow of internal migrants here. For example, a governmental decision to grant a military contract to a particular corporation or to establish a military base in a particular location will influence the direction of migratory flow. In addition, area redevelopment programs for economically depressed areas, such as that for Appalachia, reduce the number of out-migrants below what would otherwise occur.

It is obvious from the examples already cited that governments

33. James W. Brackett, "Demographic Trends and Population Policy in the Soviet Union," in U.S. Congress, 87th, *Dimensions of Soviet Economic Power* (Washington, D.C.: Government Printing Office, 1962), p. 549; Frederick A. Leedy, "Demographic Trends in the U.S.S.R.," in U.S. Congress, 93rd, *Soviet Economic Prospects for the Seventies* (Washington, D.C.: Government Printing Office, 1973), p. 451.

34. The *New York Times:* 5 May 1973 (editorial), p. 11; 10 May 1973, p. 65; 13 May 1973, p. 13.

35. Warren W. Eason, "Problems of Manpower and Industrialization in the USSR," and Demitri B. Shimkin, "Demographic Changes and Socio-economic Forces within the Soviet Union, 1939–1959," in *Population Trends in Eastern Europe, The USSR, and Mainland China* (New York: Milbank Memorial Fund, 1960), pp. 79–80, 230–37; Murray S. Weitzman et al., "Employment in the USSR: Comparative USSR–US Data," in U.S. Congress, 87th, *Dimensions of Soviet Economic Power* (Washington, D.C.: Government Printing Office, 1962), pp. 633–41; and James W. Brackett and John W. DePauw, "Population Policy and Demographic Trends in the Soviet Union," in U.S. Congress, 89th, *New Directions in the Soviet Economy* (Washington, D.C.: Government Printing Office, 1966), pp. 621–25.

have been as much concerned with regulating migration differentials as they have with controlling the absolute volume of migration. Many governments have sought to reduce ethnic heterogeneity by promoting immigration only from nations considered to be relatively similar in culture and racial composition. Many have also placed a premium on certain occupational skills. For example, the 1965 immigration legislation of the United States gives a definite preference to professional workers. As a result, the United States has been accused of perpetrating a "brain drain" from the rest of the world.

THE EFFECTIVENESS OF POPULATION POLICY

Governments throughout the world are becoming more aware of the consequences of population processes and are increasingly adapting population-influencing policies. The United States does not yet have a population policy, but President Nixon's appointment of the Commission on Population Growth and the American Future represented a first step in this direction, and there is no doubt that the Commission's recommendation to legalize abortion[36] had an important effect on the Supreme Court's 1973 decision in this regard.

Governments enact population policy with the idea that it will have a certain effect. But how are they to know that what they intend will actually come about? Ideally, the effects of a population policy should be measured by means of a controlled experiment. In the simplest form of such an experiment, areal units would be randomly divided into two groups, and the policy would be administered only to the areas within one of the two groups. Analysis of the differences between the two groups would then reveal the effects of the policy. The approximate impact of a policy may also be investigated by the statistical analysis of a so-called natural experiment. If areas exist to which the policy has been applied, and other areas exist to which it has not been applied, then a statistical analysis in which other presumably relevant variables are controlled will give some indication of the policy's actual effects. The least satisfactory way of determining the effect of a population policy is by deductive reasoning alone—that is, by imagining the results of the policy according to our general understanding of human behavior and in the light of our command of logic.

On the whole, empirical research to examine the effects of population policy has been rather infrequent. Although on a number of oc-

---

36. The Commission on Population Growth and the American Future, *Population and the American Future* (Washington, D.C.: Government Printing Office, 1972).

casions controlled experiments have been conducted to measure the effect on mortality of certain public-health policies, there have never been any to measure the effectiveness of any pro-natalist policy; nor has the impact of a pro-natalist policy ever been studied by means of a thorough statistical analysis of existing policy variation. For the most part, the effect of these policies has only been estimated from deductive arguments alone.

In the late 1960s a sharp debate arose regarding the adequacy of family-planning programs alone to reduce worldwide birth rates to a sufficiently low level. The noted demographer Kingsley Davis argued that the real problem was not that of eliminating unwanted births but that persons were motivated to want too many children. Davis further maintained that family planners, in implying that the only need was a perfect contraceptive device, avoided discussion of the possibility that "fundamental changes in social organization" were necessary prerequisites of achieving a sufficiently low level of fertility.[37]

A few controlled experiments have been done on the effect of organized birth-control campaigns. One of the earliest of such experiments, conducted in the Punjab state of India before the advent of the IUD and oral contraceptives, showed the campaign to have no measurable effect on fertility. A later Indian study, also conducted before the advent of the newer contraceptives, did show the campaign to have reduced fertility. However, the cost per prevented birth (including the cost of publicity and education) was extremely high.[38] In 1963 an elaborate experiment was conducted in a city in Taiwan to measure the effectiveness of varying degrees of intensity in disseminating information about the IUD and other contraceptives. This study provided valuable data both on the frequency of IUD insertion and on the monetary cost per insertion, depending on the intensity of the information campaign.[39]

Since in so many nations a continuation of high fertility militates against a rise in living standards and may eventually lead to higher mortality and a reduced level of living, a clear knowledge of the most efficient ways to reduce fertility is imperative. As we have seen, there has been some experimentation concerning the direct impact of organized birth-control campaigns. However, much further experimentation is necessary. For example, we need to know more about the relative effec-

37. Kingsley Davis, "Population Policy: Will Current Programs Succeed?", *Science* (10 November 1967), 163, 730–39.

38. "India: The Singur Study," and "India: The India-Harvard-Ludhiana Population Study," in *Studies in Family Planning*, No. 1 (July, 1963), pp. 1–7; and "Needed: Standardized Data from Action Programs," *Studies in Family Planning*, No. 12 (June, 1966), pp. 13–16.

39. "Cost Analysis of the Taichung Experiment," *Studies in Family Planning*, No. 10 (February, 1966), pp. 6–15.

tiveness of different types of contraceptives, the best means of communicating accurate birth-control information, and optimal ways of organizing family-planning services.

Moreover, if the availability of a perfect means of birth control will not of itself be sufficient to reduce fertility to the desired level, we must also obtain further knowledge concerning possible policies which will motivate couples to bear fewer children. Many fertility-control policies which go beyond family planning are possible, including such relatively extreme direct measures as substantial monetary incentives for having fewer children, individual child-bearing quotas, and marketable licenses for babies (a system in which a nationwide quota on average childbearing would be established, but individuals would be free to buy and sell childbearing licenses from other individuals and thus, if willing to pay the requisite price, be free to have as many babies as they wanted). Furthermore, certain changes in social structure can be instituted, such as the introduction of a social security system, programs to induce a decline in infant and child mortality, or a rise in the status of women, all of which may lead indirectly to a substantial decline in fertility.[40]

The effectiveness of some of the policies which go beyond family planning can be determined through experimentation. For example, to ascertain the effect of a reduced level of infant and child mortality on fertility, we could design a study in which a greatly improved maternal and child health service was provided for certain randomly selected experimental areas while the existing inadequate service was retained in control areas. Controlled experiments could also be used to investigate the impact of a program providing monetary incentives for couples who have refrained from bearing more than the number of children considered appropriate to the needs of society.

Other changes in social policy which might have a depressant effect on fertility probably cannot be studied by means of controlled experiments. Such changes probably include the legalization of abortion, and the introduction of social-security laws, compulsory education, and legislation restricting child labor and raising the age of marriage. Nevertheless, the effects of at least some of these can be studied by the statistical analysis of natural variations.

If fertility-control programs are to be maximally effective, much more of this type of research must be undertaken. Clearly, in the years ahead the professional student of population has an important role to play in evaluating actual and proposed population policies.

40. For a very detailed description of the various policies which have been advocated see Bernard Berelson, "Beyond Family Planning," *Science* (February, 1969), 163, 533–43.

SELECTED REFERENCES

The following constitutes a selected list of some of the more important works in the field of population study.

An encyclopedic survey of population studies is contained in Philip M. Hauser and Otis Dudley Duncan, eds., *The Study of Population: An Inventory and Appraisal* (Chicago, Ill.: University of Chicago Press, 1959).

Major works on the history of population growth include: A. M. Carr-Saunders, *World Population: Past Growth and Present Trends*, 2nd ed. (London: Frank Cass, 1964); United Nations, *The Determinants and Consequences of Population Trends* (New York: United Nations, 1953); David V. Glass and D. E. C. Eversley, eds., *Population in History* (Chicago, Ill.: Aldine, 1965); David V. Glass and Roger Revelle, eds., *Population and Social Change* (London: Edward Arnold, 1972); W. S. Rossiter, *A Century of Population Growth from the First Census of the United States to the Twelfth: 1790–1900*, reprinted edition (New York: Johnson Reprint Corp., 1966); Conrad Taeuber and Irene B. Taeuber, *The Changing Population of the United States* (New York: John Wiley, 1958); and E. A. Wrigley, *Population and History* (New York: McGraw-Hill, 1969).

Malthus's earlier and later views on the relation between population growth and increase in the means of subsistence are found respectively in Thomas Robert Malthus, *Population: The First Essay* (Ann Arbor, Mich.: Ann Arbor Paperbacks, 1959), and "A Summary View of the Principle of

Population," in Thomas Malthus et al., *Three Essays on Population* (New York: Mentor Books, 1960), pp. 13–59. Other important volumes on the relation between population and resources are Harrison Brown, *The Challenge of Man's Future* (New York: Viking Press, 1954); Georg Borgstrom, *The Hungry Planet* (New York: Macmillan, 1965); Donella Meadows et al., *The Limits to Growth* (New York: Universe Books, 1972); *The World Food Problem: A Report of the President's Science Advisory Committee*, Vols. 1 and 2 (Washington, D. C.: The White House, 1967); and Alfred Sauvy, *General Theory of Population* (New York: Basic Books, 1969).

Important books on population distribution include John I. Clarke, *Population Geography* (Oxford: Pergamon Press, 1965); Philip M. Hauser and Leo F. Schnore, eds., *The Study of Urbanization* (New York: John Wiley, 1965); and Gerald Breese *Urbanization in Newly Developing Countries* (Englewood Cliffs, N.J.: Prentice-Hall, 1966).

Two of the important works on mortality are Louis I. Dublin et al., *Length of Life: A Study of the Life Table* (New York: Ronald Press, 1949), and *Population Bulletin of the United Nations*, No. 6 (1962). Social class differences in mortality are considered thoroughly in Evelyn M. Kitagawa and Philip M. Hauser, *Differential Mortality in the United States* (Cambridge, Mass.: Harvard University Press, 1973). David M. Heer's *After Nuclear Attack: A Demographic Inquiry* (New York: Praeger, 1965) describes some of the consequences of hypothetical population losses in the United States during and as a result of a nuclear war.

Among the many important works concerned with fertility and family planning are *Population Bulletin of the United Nations*, No. 7 (1965); Wilson H. Grabill et al., *The Fertility of American Women* (New York: John Wiley, 1958); Charles F. Westoff et al., *Family Growth in Metropolitan America* (Princeton, N.J.: Princeton University Press, 1961); Norman E. Himes, *Medical History of Contraception* (New York: Gamut Press, 1963); Bernard Berelson, ed., *Family Planning and Population Programs* (Chicago, Ill.: University of Chicago Press, 1966); Pascal K. Whelpton, et al., *Fertility and Family Planning in the United States* (Princeton, N.J.: Princeton University Press, 1966); Clyde V. Kiser et al., *Trends and Variations in Fertility in the United States* (Cambridge, Mass.: Harvard University Press, 1968; Ronald Freedman and John Takeshita, *Family Planning in Taiwan* (Princeton, N.J.: Princeton University Press, 1969; S. J. Behrman et al., *Fertility and Family Planning: A World View* (Ann Arbor, Mich.: University of Michigan Press, 1970);

Stanley Johnson, *Life without Birth* (Boston, Mass.: Little, Brown and Co., 1970); Larry Bumpass and Charles Westoff, *The Later Years of Childbearing* (Princeton, N.J.: Princeton University Press, 1971); and Norman Ryder and Charles Westoff, *Reproduction in the United States: 1965* (Princeton, N.J.: Princeton University Press, 1971).

Among the major books on migration are Marcus Lee Hansen, *The Atlantic Migration, 1607 1860: A History of the Continuing Settlement of the United States* (Cambridge, Mass.: Harvard University Press, 1941); Everett S. Lee et al., *Population Redistribution and Economic Growth: United States, 1870 to 1950*, Vols. 1, 2, and 3 (Philadelphia: American Philosophical Society, 1957, 1960, and 1964); and Henry S. Shyrock, Jr., *Population Mobility within the United States* (Chicago, Ill.: Community and Family Study Center, University of Chicago, 1964).

The most significant book on the relation between population growth and economic development is Ansley J. Coale and Edgar M. Hoover, *Population Growth and Economic Development in Low-Income Countries* (Princeton, N.J.: Princeton University Press, 1958). Other important discussions are found in Harvey Leibenstein, *Economic Backwardness and Economic Growth* (New York: John Wiley, 1957), and Stephen Enke, *Economics for Development* (Englewood Cliffs, N.J.: Prentice-Hall, 1963).

The relation between population and political power is most extensively discussed in Katherine Organski and A. F. K. Organski, *Population and World Power* (New York: Alfred A. Knopf, 1961). The most comprehensive discussion of European population policies is David V. Glass, *Population Policies and Movements* (Oxford: Clarendon Press, 1940). Important viewpoints concerning population policy for the United States are contained in The Commission on Population Growth and the American Future, *Population Growth and the American Future* (Washington, D.C.: Government Printing Office, 1972).

Major studies of national populations include Kingsley Davis, *The Population of India and Pakistan* (Princeton, N.J.: Princeton University Press, 1951); Irene B. Taeuber, *The Population of Japan* (Princeton, N.J.: Princeton University Press, 1958); Frank Lorimer, *The Population of the Soviet Union: History and Prospects* (Geneva: League of Nations, 1946); Donald J. Bogue, *The Population of the United States* (New York: The Free Press, 1959); Irene B. Taeuber and Conrad Taeuber, *People of the United States in the 20th Century* (Washington, D.C.:

Government Printing Office, 1971); and Leo Orleans, *Every Fifth Child: The Population of China* (Stanford, Calif.: Stanford University Press, 1972).

Three of the chief works on demographic methodology are George W. Barclay, *Techniques of Population Analysis* (New York: John Wiley, 1958); Mortimer Spiegelman, *Introduction to Demography*, rev. ed. (Cambridge, Mass.: Harvard University Press, 1968); and Henry S. Shryock, Jacob A. Siegel, and associates, *The Methods and Materials of Demography*, Vol. I and II (Washington, D.C.: Government Printing Office, 1971).

The most important English-language periodicals devoting all or most of their contents to population are *Demography, Population Index, Population Studies, Social Biology, Studies in Family Planning, Family Planning Perspectives, International Migration Review, Population Bulletin of the United Nations, United Nations Demographic Yearbook,* and the *Current Population Reports* of the U.S. Bureau of the Census.

INDEX